TWAYNE'S WORLD AUTHORS SERIES

A Survey of the World's Literature

Sylvia E. Bowman, Indiana University

GENERAL EDITOR

ITALY

Carlo Golino, University of Massachusetts, Boston

EDITOR

St. Thomas Aquinas

TWAS 408

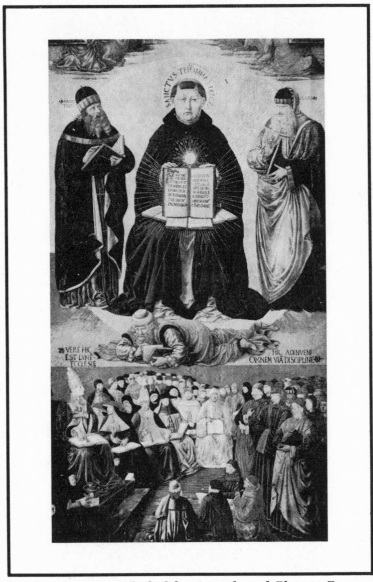

St. Thomas Aquinas flanked by Aristotle and Plato in Benozzo Gozzoli's *Le triomphe de Saint Thomas* (Paris, Musée du Louvre).

ST. THOMAS AQUINAS

By RALPH McINERNY
University of Notre Dame

TWAYNE PUBLISHERS
A DIVISION OF G. K. HALL & CO., BOSTON

Library of Congress Cataloging in Publication Data

McInerny, Ralph M
    St. Thomas Aquinas.

    (Twayne's world authors series ; TWAS 408 : Italy)
    Bibliography: pp. 183–89
    Includes index.
    1. Thomas Aquinas, Saint, 1225?–1274.
B765.T54M244   230′.2′0924   76–25959
ISBN 0–8057–6248–5

Filiabus filiisque meis:

Cathy, Mary, Anne,
David, Beth and Dan

Contents

About the Author

Ralph McInerny was born in Minneapolis and was educated at the St. Paul Seminary, the University of Minnesota and Laval University. He has been a member of the Department of Philosophy at the University of Notre Dame since 1955. He was a Fulbright Research Scholar at the University of Louvain in 1959–1960. A past president of the American Catholic Philosophical Association, he is Associate Editor of *The New Scholasticism*. Among his publications are *The Logic of Analogy, Studies in Analogy, A History of Western Philosophy*, Volume 1, *From the Beginnings to Plotinus*, Volume 2, *From Augustine to Ockham*, and *Thomism in an Age of Renewal*.

Preface

In this book, I have aspired to write an introduction to the thought of a man who for some seven hundred years has been a major influence in philosophy and theology. I say *aspired*, because, far from being an easy thing, something one might do at odd moments and with but half one's mind engaged, writing an introduction is a difficult thing. The reader will detect, I trust, a note of anguished sincerity in that remark. I wanted to make the thought of Thomas Aquinas attractive, but attractive for the right reasons. So I have at least suggested the structure of the arguments he uses to arrive at his positions. I wanted the book to be comprehensive, yet I hoped to avoid thinness. Most important, I have tried to present Thomas in such a way that my reader would quickly leave me and go to the works of Aquinas himself.

Perhaps no book could have accomplished all this. The structure I have used is at once natural and unusual. The reader will swiftly see how reliant Thomas was on his predecessors; many of his works are commentaries on earlier ones. Why not present the thought of Thomas in close connection with its major sources? This method seemed a good idea and presented no insuperable difficulties as I put it into effect. The Table of Contents will convince the reader that I have managed to cover a wide range of topics without grievous overlapping. Of course, my eye has been mainly on what Thomas made of his sources rather than on the sources themselves. Nonetheless, my procedure should enable the reader to appreciate both Thomas's continuity with earlier thought and his creative independence of it.

The translations in the text are all mine. This is not because of any negative judgment on the translations that are listed in the Bibliography. The truth is, I do not have any opinion at all about the vast majority of those translations—except to wish that they were not necessary. Thomas's Latin is the least difficult thing about reading him and anyone with the slightest gift for languages could learn to read the *Summa theologiae*, say, in short order. In any case, in drafting these chapters, I have turned Thomas into English whenever I wanted to quote him. I might have replaced these with the more careful translations of others before sending the book to the printer, but I decided against this for several reasons. First, there is a sameness of style in the quotations now, and of course I do not regard sameness as a *literary* achievement. Second, I deliberately rendered Thomas loosely, in the interests of accuracy, dreading that fidelity to the text which can turn it into a dead letter. I have taken no distorting liberties, and perhaps I overstate my looseness and underestimate the dullness of the English I have made Thomas speak. Finally, it was a great practical advantage to have done my own translating. I was saved the enormous bother of requesting permission to use the translations of others.

Over the more than two decades of my academic career, during which I have been a constant reader of Aquinas, I have watched his philosophical stock rise and fall and now see it begin to rise again. Once he was a household word in Catholic universities and colleges; then he became almost an unknown figure. But elsewhere he was read closely and learned from. Perhaps the two events are not unconnected. These minor fluctuations give no true indication of the continuing surge of his influence. The year 1974 marked the seven hundredth anniversary of the death of Thomas Aquinas. The global character of the commemorations was overwhelming. There were countless meetings, conventions, symposia held in his honor. An international meeting held in Rome and Naples in April 1974 brought delegates from the ends of the earth. Special issues of learned journals were devoted to the thought of Thomas. I had hoped to finish this book in time for it to appear during that anniversary year. That was not to be. Perhaps it can play some small part in the beginning of the next seven hundred years of Thomas's historical influence.

RALPH McINERNY

University of Notre Dame

Chronology

1216	Order of Preachers confirmed by Pope Honorius III.
1217	Dominicans arrive in Paris.
1224/5	Thomas born at Rocca Secca.
1230/1	Thomas becomes a Benedictine oblate at Monte Cassino.
1239	Thomas studies at Naples.
1244	Thomas joins Dominicans and is held captive by his family for a year.
1245–1248	Thomas at Dominican convent of St. Jacques in Paris.
1248–1252	Thomas studies under Albert the Great in Cologne.
1250/1	Thomas is ordained priest.
1252–1256	Thomas studies theology at Paris.
1256–1259	Thomas teaches theology at Paris. Writes expositions of Boethius's *On the Trinity* and *De hebdomadibus*.
1259–1265	Thomas in Naples and Orvieto. Completes *Summa Against the Gentiles*. Writes Part One of *Summa theologiae*.
1265–1268	Thomas at Santa Sabina in Rome, then in Viterbo. Writing commentaries on Aristotle.
1269–1272	Thomas again teaches theology at Paris. Writes against the Latin Averroists; completes Part Two of *Summa theologiae*.
1272	Thomas assigned to Naples. Writes first ninety questions of Part Three of *Summa theologiae*.
1274	March 7: Thomas dies at Fossanova.
1277	March 7: Thomas condemned at Paris.
1323	Thomas is canonized.
1325	Paris condemnation revoked.

CHAPTER 1

Works and Days

TOMMASO d'Aquino was born in the family castle at Rocca Secca in Southern Italy in 1225, the youngest son of a large family. The first records of the family date from the 9th century; the title of count was held from the 10th to the 12th century; one of Tommaso's ancestors was abbot of Monte Cassino, which, like Rocca Secca, lies midway between Rome and Naples. Today the traveller moves swiftly between these two cities on a magnificent *autostrada*, and, when his eye is caught by the white eminence of the great Benedictine monastery, rebuilt since World War II when it was bombed by the Allies, he may be tempted, as the blue and white highway signs announce Aquino, to turn off and seek out such physical reminders as remain of the origins of the man we know as St. Thomas Aquinas. As is often the case with great men, nothing the traveller finds will suggest any inevitability in the rise to world importance of Thomas.

I *Youth and First Studies*

The area of Italy in which Thomas was born was at the time part of the Kingdom of Sicily; during Thomas's youth the ruler of the kingdom was the Emperor Frederick II. Landolfo, the father of Thomas, together with his older sons, soldiered for the emperor and thus they were caught up in the disputes between Frederick and the Papal States, which lay just to the north. That the family of the future Common Doctor of the Roman Catholic Church should thus have been arrayed against the Pope as temporal ruler has possibilities of irony. As we shall see, Thomas himself was to spend years in the courts of various popes. This youngest son of a feudal noble family in decline was not destined to participate in the family's military exploits.

He did, however, follow one family tradition. At the age of five he became a Benedictine oblate at Monte Cassino.

As the term suggests, an oblate was one offered by his parents and the offering involved the promise that Thomas would live the life of a monk according to the Rule of St. Benedict. This does not mean, of course, that Thomas became a monk at the age of five. The idea was that he would be educated at the monastery and, when he had reached the age of discretion, make a choice for or against the religious life. Only much later could solemn vows be taken. There are grounds for thinking that his family had high hopes for the small boy they brought to the neighborhood monastery, that they saw in him a future abbot of Monte Cassino, with everything that such a position involved. Indeed, it is not unlikely that the then abbot, Landolfo Sinnibaldo, was a distant relative.[1]

When we read of Thomas brought at so tender an age to a monastery, we may form the impression of a tranquil if odd childhood spent acquiring the rudiments of learning and of course devoted to the work and prayer that are the Benedictine ideal. But Monte Cassino did not have to wait until our century to be caught in the pincers of war. The squabble between Pope and Emperor intensified—Frederick II was excommunicated in 1239; his adversary had otherworldly weapons as well as troops —and Monte Cassino was threatened. Indeed it was occupied by Sicilian troops and, though they celebrated no vespers of the ominous kind, many monks were sent into exile. The monastery became a rather dangerous place to be and, in 1239, Thomas was taken away by his parents and sent to the University of Naples to continue his studies.

Thus, one possible career was shelved and, while still young, Thomas was put upon a different path, one that was doubtless suggested by the first signs of brilliance exhibited at Monte Cassino. As to what precisely Thomas learned at the monastery we are left to conjecture. Certainly it was there that he learned Latin, since this would have been required for participation in the liturgical activities of the monastery. Thomas's mother tongue was a Neapolitan dialect. Scripture, the Latin Fathers, and Benedictine authors would doubtless have made up his reading fare—the training, in short, of a future monk.

The University of Naples was founded by Frederick II in 1224, and the emperor was still alive when Thomas arrived in Naples in 1239. Thomas became a student of the liberal arts at a university whose founder was a patron of Mohammedan and Jewish as well as of Christian scholars. Frederick's patronage brought it about that Naples was to play a considerable role in the introduction into the Latin West of ancient and Islamic learning, a major feature of the intellectual milieu in which Thomas would spend his life.

The seven liberal arts were divided into two groups: the *trivium*, consisting of grammar, rhetoric, and dialectic; and the *quadrivium*, consisting of arithmetic, geometry, astronomy, and music.[2] Who were the teachers of Thomas Aquinas in Naples? The matter has never been satisfactorily settled, although William of Tocco, an early biographer, says that Thomas studied grammar and logic with a Master Martin and natural philosophy under Master Peter of Ireland.[3] It seems probable that Thomas was put into acquaintance with the works of Aristotle and of commentaries on them by Avicenna, a fact that would indicate that the new learning made adherence to the traditional curriculum of the liberal arts tenuous at best. What is of the greatest importance is the likelihood that Thomas began at Naples the reading of Aristotle and the Arabic commentaries on him, for it was Thomas, more than any other 13th-century figure, who would weave Aristotle and the other more traditional strands of intellectual influence into a new and coherent synthesis.

Another fact of extreme importance in these Naples years is that Thomas made the acquaintance of members of the new Order of St. Dominic.[4] Given papal approval in 1216, this new religious group, the Order of Preachers, was like the Franciscans in its emphasis on poverty and obedience, but was distinguished by its emphasis on the intellectual life. The master general of the Dominicans visited Naples, as he did other university towns, and men of the stature of Albert the Great, under whom Thomas would later study at Cologne, entered the Order. Thomas too decided to join.

This decision did not please his brothers. The father of the house had died, but Thomas's mother, Teodora, unhappy that her youngest son had joined the Dominicans, communicated her

unhappiness to Thomas's older brothers, who were then cam-
paigning with the army of Frederick II. As if sensing trouble, the
Dominicans had sent Thomas away, bound for the north. He
was snatched from the band of travelling friars and incarcerated
in a family castle, perhaps for as long as a year. It may be that it
was during this period that Thomas wrote two works, a treatise
on fallacies and another on modal propositions, works that
exhibit both the youth of their author and the flavor of the
logical instruction he had received at Naples. When his family
became convinced that Thomas could not be dissuaded from his
decision, they released him to return to his brothers in religion.[5]

It was in 1243 or 1244 that Thomas became a Dominican
novice in Naples. After his release by his family, he was sent to
the house of the Order in Paris. Thomas's whereabouts from 1245
to 1248 have been a matter of dispute, but the safest opinion
would seem to be that he spent those years studying in Paris,
attending lectures in theology. It is beyond dispute that he spent
the years from 1248 to 1252 in Cologne, where he studied in
the new *Studium Generale* of his Order under Albert the Great.[6]
That Thomas was Albert's assistant seems attested to by the
fact that Albert's lectures on Aristotle's *Nicomachean Ethics* were
taken down in Thomas's hand. Albert was a man of prodigious
learning and breadth of interest. There can be little doubt that
he had a tremendous impact on his gifted student, though it is
equally true that the mature thought of Thomas differs from
that of his teacher.

II   *Paris: 1252–1259*

The University of Paris, where Thomas Aquinas was to spend
a significant portion of his life, was granted its charter in 1200
and is thought to have grown out of such 12th-century institutions as the Cathedral school of Notre Dame and the theological
schools of the monasteries of St. Victor and Mont Ste. Geneviève.
Its Faculty of Arts was not unlike the one Thomas had attended
at the University of Naples. A student was admitted at the age
of fifteen and after six years of study became a Bachelor of
Arts; then, after explicating classical texts under the surveillance
of a master, the right to teach (*licentia docendi*) was granted
and he became *Magister Artium*, a Master of Arts.[7]

The Faculty of Arts was a preparatory school for three others, the Faculty of Law, the Faculty of Medicine, and the Faculty of Theology. At Paris, it was the last which was the best and the most important. When a Master of Arts became a student in theology, eight years lay between him and the baccalaureate. At that point, he was a biblical bachelor who for at least a year was required to lecture on Scripture under the direction of the master to whom he was assigned; for two years after that his task was to comment on the *Sentences* of Peter Lombard, which was an accepted compilation of theological doctrine. After further academic work he was granted a *licentia docendi* and was received as a Master of Theology into the university corporation.

As this suggests, the university was patterned on the guilds, and the master/apprentice relationship was geared toward admission to full standing in the profession. Originally, the masters were secular or diocesan priests, by and large, a fact that was to have its importance later when the presence of Dominican and Franciscan masters was objected to.

The manner of teaching at Paris, in both the Arts and Theology faculties, was twofold, comprising lecture and dispute (*lectio* and *disputatio*). Lecturing, as the etymology of the term suggests, meant reading and commenting on a classical text. The disputations were less tied to texts and permitted the developed expositions of the thought of a master. The so-called Quodlibetal Disputes, disputes on what you will, were held twice a year, at Christmas and Easter, and here the master was subject to any and all interventions from his audience.

So much for the mechanics of the setting in which Thomas began his teaching career. In order to understand the direction and achievement of his thought, something must be known of the remarkable changes which had been taking place in higher learning and which came to a head in the 13th century. When we look backward from the year 1200 onto the intellectual activity of the preceding centuries, we see many peaks and valleys. If on the far horizon we see Mount Augustine, a closer peak would be Boethius, a minor foothill Cassiodorus. A valley, then, even a ravine, until, in the Carolingian period, Alcuin, Rhabanus Maurus, and, principally, John Scotus Erigena would stand out. In the 12th century, the landscape becomes suddenly

mountainous: Anselm of Canterbury, Peter Abelard, Hugh of St.
Victor, the School of Chartres, Bernard of Clairvaux. The 12th
century might have been our Alps if it had not been followed by
the 13th. The great difference between these two centuries may
be seen in the sudden introduction into the Latin West of a whole
library of works from ancient Greece and from the intervening
Jewish and Islamic cultures. The translation of such works,
already begun in the 12th century, at Toledo and in Sicily, was
to provide the 13th with a vast new set of sources for speculation
and with a whole new menu of philosophical and theological
problems. As we shall see, one of Thomas Aquinas's greatest
claims on our attention lies in the fact that he met and mastered
this new literature and synthesized it with what had gone before
in the Latin world, a synthesis that was not a concordance, an
eclectic assembling of disparate elements, but a whole that was
a good deal more than the sum of its parts.

One unacquainted with the vagaries that attend the trans-
mission of literary works might imagine that men of the 12th and
11th centuries, being that much closer to the ancient Greeks
than we are, would have known at least as much and probably
more of their literature. The fact is that Plato was known only
in an incomplete translation of his *Timaeus* (even in the 13th
century only the *Phaedo* and the *Meno* were added to the list);
Aristotle was known through Boethius's translation of the
Categories and *On Interpretation*. Of course, much Platonism
and Neoplatonism was known indirectly through Augustine, the
Pseudo-Dionysius, and other Fathers of the Church. It would be
too much to say that for centuries philosophy was almost
identified with logic, but it is certain that there was no clear
conception of philosophy as having the scope that it had had for
the Greeks. Consequently, there was no clear notion of the
demarcation between theology and philosophy.

Greek philosophy passed to the Islamic world through Syria,
into Egypt, and then along the southern shore of the Mediterranean until, where Christianity and Islam came into contact, in
Spain and in the seaports of the Kingdom of Sicily, Greek works
and Arabic works began to be translated into Latin. Almost
simultaneously, via Constantinople, contact was made with
original Greek texts. When the works of Aristotle came into

the West from Islam, they were accompanied by the interpretations and commentaries of Islamic thinkers, of whom the most important were Avicenna (Ibn Sina), a Persion by birth who died in 1037, and Averroes (Ibn Roschd), a native of Cordova who died in 1198. Two influential Jewish thinkers were Salomon Ibn Gabirol (d. 1070), who lived in Saragossa and was known to the Latins as Avicebron; and Moses Maimonides, who was born in Cordova and died in Egypt in 1205.[8]

One significance of the Islamic and Jewish authors mentioned lies in the fact that they had confronted, a century or two earlier, the very problems that were to exercise the minds of Christians from the 13th century onward. When the philosophy of the pagan Greeks was seen in its full scope, it appeared to present not only a total vision of reality, and of man's place in it, but one that rivaled the vision held by men of faith. In quite different ways, Avicenna and Averroes tried to make Greek thought, which for them was a curious amalgam of Aristotle and Neoplatonism, square with the truth as revealed in the Koran. So too Moses Maimonides, in his magnificent *Guide for the Perplexed*, was anxious to establish the relations between philosophical speculation and the Bible. The great task in the Latin West was to find some modus vivendi between the influx of new literature and the truths of Christianity in their traditional form. This entailed, of course, assimilation, commentaries, interpretation. One of its effects was that for the first time a clear conception of what theology is developed. That is to say, the believer did not simply account for the new learning in terms of an existent theology, ready to hand; in accounting for the new learning, he devised a new theology.

We will mention here three examples of the sort of problem the believer faced. The writings of Aristotle appear to contain the claims that the world is eternal, that there is no personal immortality, and that God is not concerned with the world, that is, a denial of providence. All these claims are contrary to Christian belief. What then, apart from obscurantism, could the Christian reaction be to such a philosopher as Aristotle? At least three general sorts of reaction are possible and each was exemplified in the 13th century. First, one might say that Aristotle was right and that Christian belief was also right, despite the fact that they contradicted each other. Second, one might say that the faith was right and therefore that Aristotle was wrong and ought to be condemned. Third, and this was the approach of Thomas Aquinas, one might say: let us read Aristotle with great care in order to see if he does indeed teach what the Arabic commentaries say he teaches. It may be that these commentaries are not always historically accurate in what they ascribe to Aristotle. Furthermore, where they are accurate, we can still ask whether Aristotle thought his claims to be certain truths or merely probable opinions.

Perhaps this will suffice to indicate the kind of charged, even revolutionary, intellectual milieu into which Thomas Aquinas was introduced. It should be added that, along with Aristotle, Neoplatonic works also became available in the West, though in disguised forms. The so-called *Book of Causes* (*Liber de causis*) is fashioned from Proclus's *Elements of Theology*, a discovery first made by Thomas Aquinas when the full work of Proclus came into his hands.[9] The so-called *Theology of Aristotle* consisted of extracts from the *Enneads* of Plotinus. Thus, Greek thought, principally Aristotelian, but also Neoplatonic, together with Islamic and Jewish thought, flowed suddenly into the West and created an unparalleled challenge to and opportunity for such men as Thomas Aquinas.

When we left Thomas, he was studying under Albert the Great at the Dominican house of studies in Cologne. The year is 1252. Thomas is next sent by his Order to continue his theological studies at the University of Paris, where, we have seen, he had already spent three years. Now, according to the procedure sketched above, Thomas should have begun his teaching career at Paris by commenting on Scripture and then gone on to comment on the *Sentences* of Peter Lombard. The first stage of his career is a matter of some doubt because none of his scriptural commentaries would seem to date from this time. The second stage is amply attested to by his exposition of the *Sentences*. Thomas received his *licentia docendi* in 1256, but prior to this he wrote the *De ente et essentia* (*On Being and Essence*) and the *De principiis naturae* (*On the Principles of Nature*). He also wrote two polemical works addressed to a situation which prevented his being accepted as a Master of Theology in the Faculty of Theology until August 15, 1257.

We have already alluded to the resentment felt by the masters of theology who were not Dominicans or Franciscans toward those who were. The leader of the opposition to the mendicant friars was William of St. Amour whose tracts against the friars demonstrate the passion with which the dispute was carried on. Appealing to that last refuge of the viewer with alarm, William professed to see in the phenomenon of the friars a clear sign of the impending end of the world. Thomas's defense of the religious life we shall consider later. Other works of Thomas dating from this time are his two commentaries on Boethius (the *De trinitate* and the *De hebdomadibus*); the *Disputed Questions on Truth;* the commentary on Matthew's Gospel; and some *Quodlibetal Questions.* Thus, when Thomas left Paris in 1259, at the age of thirty-four, he had already produced a good number of writings. There were many more to come.

III *Italy: 1259–1268*

In recent years, to counter what has been thought to be too exclusive and misleading an emphasis on his philosophy, we have been reminded that Thomas Aquinas was primarily a theologian. The next period of his life serves to remind us that even more primarily he was a Dominican.

After attending a conference of his Order at Valenciennes, Thomas was ordered back to Italy, where for nearly ten years he exercised a roving role as preacher general. It is often said that Thomas returned to Italy in order to fulfill some function in the papal court, but there does not seem to be any evidence to support this. What the evidence does support is that he taught theology in a series of Dominican houses in various parts of Italy. This teaching began at the monastery in Anagni, south of Rome; in 1261 he began to teach at the monastery in Orvieto; in 1265 he became head of the house of studies in Rome at the monastery of Santa Sabina; from 1267 he was in Viterbo.

Besides these teaching assignments, Thomas in his role of preacher general visited Naples, Orvieto, Perugia, Todi, and Lucca, as well as the cities already mentioned. There is even a not very substantiated but still intriguing suggestion that he visited London. It was during his assignments in Orvieto, Rome, and Viterbo, particularly the first and last, that Thomas was in the vicinity of the papal court and, though he held no official position, he would no doubt have benefitted from its proximity. Pope Urban IV had his court in Orvieto and he was a great patron of learning. Furthermore, Albert the Great was then in Orvieto, resident at the papal court, and, even more significant, William of Moerbeke, a Flemish Dominican, indefatigable translator from the Greek who was to end his life as bishop of Corinth, was also at Orvieto. At Thomas's request, so it is said, William began to translate and revise earlier translations of Aristotle.[10] It was during this Italian period that Aquinas began one of the tasks which was to occupy him on and off for the rest of his life. We have already seen how potentially disruptive of orthodoxy the new wave of literature seemed. There was an urgent need to study and assess these works of Aristotle together with the Arabic commentaries on them. Apparently with papal approval and aid, Thomas undertook his share of this work and, to do it well, he wanted translations as accurate as possible. No one was better equipped to provide them than William of Moerbeke. In a purely literary sense, his translations are unexciting, even dull; the goal he set himself was to provide as exact a transliteration as possible, and so well did he succeed in this task that his Latin translations are sometimes employed in establishing critical editions of the Greek text. With such accurate translations at his disposal, Thomas began composing expositions or commentaries on Aristotle. During the period we are now considering, he commented on the *Metaphysics* (from 1266 onward) and perhaps the First Book of *On the Soul* as well as on the short works *On Sense and the Sensed* and *On Memory*.

As professor of theology, Thomas held disputes during this period and the result was his *Disputed Questions on the Power of God* (1265–1268) and *On Spiritual Creatures* (1268). He compiled the *Catena aurea* (Golden Chain) of comments on the Gospels, commented on Isaiah and Jeremiah, and wrote his commentary on *The Divine Names* of Pseudo-Dionysius.

The first of his great summaries of Catholic doctrine, the *Summa contra gentiles*, which he had begun in Paris, was

completed in Italy prior to 1265. His *Summa theologiae* was
begun during this Italian period and the First Part was written
from 1266 to 1268.

It is extremely difficult to date with certainty all the commentaries on or expositions of Aristotle's works that Thomas
wrote. Parts of some of them are reports (*reportationes*), that is,
in effect, a listener's notes on Thomas's lectures. Others were
dictated by Aquinas to the secretaries who had been assigned
him, fellow Dominicans, this convenience explained in part by
the fact that Thomas's own handwriting, of which we have
samples, came justifiably to be known as the *littera inintelligibilis,*
the unreadable script. It seems to be the case that Thomas
engaged in this work of unravelling the text of Aristotle as
best he could while carrying on any number of other projects.
Thus it is that scholars hold that some commentaries on
Aristotle begun during this Italian period were completed only
later or not at all. What is certain is that this work went on
almost to the end of Thomas's life and that it had a profound
influence on his own thought. Besides the works already mentioned, and without concern now for dating them, Thomas commented on the following works of Aristotle: *Nicomachean
Ethics, Politics* (Books 1-3), *On Interpretation* (through 19b30),
*Posterior Analytics, On the Heavens, Meteorology, On Genera-
tion and Corruption,* and the *Physics.* The nature and significance
of these commentaries on Aristotle will occupy us later.

IV   *Paris: 1269–1272*

Perhaps at the end of 1268, Thomas was sent back to Paris
to occupy once more one of the two Dominican chairs of theology
at the university. Anyone tempted to think of the medieval university as peaceful and untroubled would do well to consider
the University of Paris during Thomas's second tenure there as
professor of theology. We have already seen the dispute between
the secular and mendicant masters; there were as well somewhat
ill-tempered disagreements among the theologians of his Order
concerning matters in which Thomas became involved because
of inquiries from the Dominican master general. There were
attacks on Thomas emanating from the Faculty of Arts, whose
rector, Siger of Brabant, was an adherent of what Van Steen-

berghen has called "Heterodox Aristotelianism."[11] There were strikes, and classes were suspended. All in all, a typical university situation when such institutions are in their more creative moments.

Heterodox Aristotelianism provided an occasion for Thomas to clarify his own interpretations and assessments of Aristotle as well as of his Islamic commentators. He wrote his short works *On the Eternity of the World* and *On the Unicity of the Intellect*. In the former, he maintained that, on the level of philosophy or science, it was impossible to decide whether or not the world and time had a beginning. Nonetheless, since faith teaches that the world and time began, Thomas thus avoids the two-truth theory, that which maintains that something can be true in philosophy yet false for faith. In the latter work, he contested at length a reading of Aristotle favored by Averroes and some Parisian Aristotelians, according to which there is but one mind or intellect for all men. As we shall see, this work provides a good test of the claim that, in reading Aristotle, Thomas was not so much interested in what Aristotle taught as in what he could be made to say that would be in agreement with Christian faith. Thomas is here moving on the level of exegesis and claiming that his reading of Aristotle is supported by the text, while the other is not.

If Thomas was thus trying on the one hand to rescue Aristotle from inept and dangerous interpreters, on the other he was forced to defend his own manner of doing theology, which involved deploying his extensive understanding of and agreement with Aristotle. This manner went against the grain of traditional theologizing and led Thomas to be more critical of Augustine than had hitherto seemed possible. The substance of these controversies, as they emerge in the writings of Thomas, will concern us in subsequent chapters.

A work of Thomas written during this period in response to the renewed attack on the mendicants in the university is his *On the Perfection of the Spiritual Life*. He was, as has been indicated earlier, continuing his commentaries on the writings of Aristotle. He commented on the *Book of Causes*, which, thanks to a translation of Proclus's *Elements of Theology* he now had, he was able to identify as selections from Proclus. He wrote the

Second Part of the *Summa theologiae*. He may have begun the unfinished *Compendium theologiae* at this time. He commented on the Gospel of St. John and the Epistles of St. Paul. Among the disputed questions he engaged in at this time are those concerned with the soul, with evil, with the virtues. and with the Incarnation. Finally, the *Quodlibetal Questions* I-VI date from this sojourn in Paris when he occupied a Dominican chair in theology.[12]

When one considers the electric atmosphere of the university during this three-year period, when one thinks of the controversies in which Thomas was involved, his output seems almost incredibly prodigious. At one time, all or most of the commentaries on Aristotle were assigned to this period of Thomas's career, but even if we make allowance for beginnings in Italy, the fact that he may have completed a large proportion of the work on many of these during his second Paris professorate, along with other writings, confronts us with a phenomenon that is not much altered by the theory recently propounded that Thomas was provided with a staff of secretaries to whom he dictated.[13]

V *Italy: 1272–1274*

Thomas's next assignment was as regent of studies in Naples, and in the summer of 1272, together with his fellow Dominican and secretary, Reginald of Piperno, Thomas began the long walk south. It should be noted, incidentally, when we consider Thomas's extensive travels, that as a Dominican he was obliged to journey on foot. The modern traveller who flies or drives between the cities that show up on the map of Thomas's life may find it difficult to imagine all that hiking about the continent. Due to delays, Thomas and Reginald did not arrive in Naples until September.

Thomas thus returned to the community where he had himself entered the Dominican Order. His task was to set up a house of studies that would be connected with the University of Naples. Thus his teaching career, as well as his writing, continued. The Third Part of the *Summa theologiae*, through Question 90, which is as far as Thomas got, was written in Naples. The work of commenting on Aristotle continued into this last

period of Thomas's life. His commentary on Isaiah also dates
from this period as does his exposition of the Psalms, which is
incomplete.

There now occurred an event of a most puzzling nature.[14]
Thomas ceased to write and teach, and, to the inquiries of his
friend Reginald of Piperno, replied that after the things he had
seen, everything he had written now seemed to him as so much
chaff. This final phrase would seem to connect with one or
two other events that are reported by early biographers and in
the canonization process. One night, after a period during which
Thomas had been fasting and praying because he could not
make sense of a scriptural passage on which he had to comment,
Reginald heard Thomas in conversation in his cell. After a time,
Thomas summoned his secretary and began again the dictation
of his commentary. Persistent questioning by Reginald drew the
answer that Peter and Paul had visited Thomas to discuss the
difficult passage with him. There are other stories, too, among
them one where Thomas was seen praying in church, his feet
hovering some distance above the floor. During one of these
events, we may surmise, Thomas was granted a vision, after
which his own efforts to understand and explain divine things
seemed pointless and absurd. The Catholic view of life, as we
shall see Thomas explain it, holds that on this earth we are *in via*,
on the way to a destiny that is wholly out of proportion to our
natural desires and deserts. Faith is the dark knowledge we now
have of the luminous reality that awaits us, and in the next life, *in
patria*, faith will give way to a kind of direct seeing of God that
will constitute our eternal beatitude. In the *Summa theologiae*,
Thomas devoted a question to the discussion of such mystical
rapture as he seems to have experienced himself,[15] but the discussion is, as usual, wholly impersonal, based on the Scriptures
and the Fathers. With respect to Paul's remark about having
been caught up into the third heaven,[16] Thomas held that Paul
saw God in his essence and not merely in some likeness or
similitude. If Thomas himself had a comparable experience, his
negative estimate of his lifework is no doubt understandable,
but it is important to remember from what vantage point it
is that such a prodigious achievement as his looks like chaff.

This episode reminds us that with Thomas Aquinas we are

dealing not only with a great mind and with one of the greatest and most influential Italian authors, but with a religious, a Dominican, a saint. Sprung from a noble lineage, Thomas throughout his life had contact with the great of this world, with emperors and kings and popes. There is a well-known account of Thomas at table with the king of France suddenly hitting on a refutation of the Manichean heresy, and on the table, in that order. Before leaving Naples for the last time, he had a meeting with Charles II. As for churchmen, he had the acquaintance of several popes and presumably many cardinals and bishops. For all that, the picture of Thomas that emerges from the accounts of those who knew him is primarily one of a humble and obedient friar. The religious life, the Dominican life, naturally involves a commitment to make a special and life-long effort to observe the counsels of perfection as well as the commandments, to strive for sanctity. Everything else in Thomas's life was subordinate to this calling and unless we recognize this we simply do not have an accurate picture of the man.

At the beginning of 1274, Thomas set out for Lyons where a general council of the Church was to be held which he had been ordered to attend. There is reason to believe that he had been in poor health in Naples. On the way north, he visited a niece at Maenza and was stricken again. After a few days he was moved to the Cistercian monastery at Fossanova and it was there, on the morning of March 7, at the age of forty-nine, that Thomas Aquinas died.

Benedictine oblate, lay student at the University of Naples, Dominican student and then professor at the University of Paris and in various houses of study of his Order—that in its bare bones is the life of Thomas. We have seen how his writings emerged naturally out of his activities as a teacher. In many respects, there is nothing wholly distinctive about such a life at such a time. Other masters of theology produced bodies of writing as extensive, other theologians concerned themselves with the newly introduced writings of Aristotle, with the Arabic commentaries, with various Neoplatonic and Jewish authors. Nor was Thomas the first to write summary works of theology which attempted to incorporate this new knowledge. To discover what is distinctive in the work of Thomas Aquinas, we must go beyond the format of his writings, their occasion and purpose, their sheer bulk.

We have mentioned that Thomas was principally a theologian. This is a valid reminder and it will be necessary for us to see what his vision of the nature, scope, and method of theology was as well as to evaluate his substantive contributions to this discipline. But it must also be emphasized that Thomas was a philosopher. His commentaries on Aristotle are not as such theological works: they are philosophical works. Compared with his independent philosophical writings, polemical and otherwise, they enable us to comprehend his basic philosophical outlook and to see the contributions he made to philosophy. The fact that he wished to understand Aristotle in order, later, to make use of this understanding in a theological context should not blind us to the autonomous character of that preliminary stage. Furthermore, his conception of theology entailed that, in the course of theological investigation, clarification of preliminary philosophical concepts be made. The sources of our knowledge of the philosophy of Thomas Aquinas are not merely his commentaries on philosophical works nor his independent philosophical writings; the theological writings of Thomas are treasure houses of philosophical clarifications.

In what follows, we shall be considering the writings of Thomas under four major headings. Since one of his major tasks was to assimilate philosophical literature, old and new, we shall consider his relation to the thought of Aristotle, to the thought of Boethius, and to Platonism and Neoplatonism. We use these abstract designations since it is not known with certainty how much of Plato Thomas had read. In any case, he could not read him in the Greek and there was precious little available in Latin translation. Finally, we shall consider Thomas as theologian.

These divisions of our labor have both advantages and disadvantages. While they do not permit us to approach Thomas chronologically as such, it does happen that his commentaries on Boethius are early and can naturally be associated with the works *On the Principles of Nature* and *On Being and Essence*. As for Aristotle, there is no chance of considering the commentaries and allied independent writings as confined to any one period of Thomas's life. As we have already seen, throughout his life Thomas was fashioning his commentaries on Aristotle. The major convenience of our approach is that it enables us to speak first, in Chapters 2 to 4, of the philosophy of Aquinas, leaving the discussion of his theology till later.

CHAPTER 2

Thomas Aquinas and Aristotle

I Aristotle Goes West

IT has been said that without Thomas, Aristotle would be
mute; it can equally well be said that without Aristotle,
Thomas would be unintelligible. Like so many of his contemporaries, St. Thomas refers to Aristotle as "the Philosopher," but
his use of the appellation cannot be explained simply in terms
of a convention of the times.

Although it is in many respects impossible to speak of even
the early portion of the Middle Ages without mentioning Aristotle's influence, it is important to see how different that
influence was before and after, say, 1200. In the early Middle
Ages, Aristotle was known as the author of the logical works
that had been translated by and commented on by Boethius.
Only by remembering this will we be able to survive our surprise
at hearing Plato rather than Aristotle spoken of as a physicist
or philosopher of nature. These early medievals had a partial
translation of Plato's *Timaeus*, whereas the natural writings of
Aristotle, which form the bulk of his oeuvre, were not yet known.
It must have been suspected that the handful of logical treatises
which served as school textbooks were but the tip of the
Aristotelian iceberg—after all, the titles, at least, of other works
were known—but when the full scope of Aristotle's production
became known, when all the treatises we associate with the
name of Aristotle came into the West almost en masse, the
image of the iceberg is aptly suggestive of the disruptive, dis-
quieting, and awesome effect they had.[1]

For the works of Aristotle to have had this impact, they had
first of all to be translated. This work of rendering Aristotle
legible began in Spain during the 12th century, notably in
Toledo under the aegis of one Archbishop Raymond. In Spain,

30

the Christian, Moslem, and Jewish cultures were, however uneasily, juxtaposed. It is thought that the works of Aristotle were first translated into the vernacular Spanish and thence into Latin, and, when we consider that they had found their way into Arabic via a previous Syriac translation, we can appreciate how easily inaccuracies could creep into the text. To the vagaries of this trek through the world south of the Mediterranean must be added the further complication that Aristotle came into the West escorted by Moslem interpreters, with the result that Aristotle's meaning was often identified with what such great scholars as Avicenna and Averroes said it was.

The Aristotle who had been largely inaccessible to the West was not to be confined to a single mode of entry once his advent finally took place. At the papal court, the *studium curiae*, where Thomas spent the years 1261–65 and 1267–68, a Flemish Dominican, William of Moerbeke, was occupied in translations from the Greek. This remarkable man, who was later to be bishop of Corinth, was responsible for many translations from the Greek, and it is said that Thomas urged him to provide versions of Aristotle more accurate than those coming from the Iberian peninsula.[2] William obliged and so accurate and literal were his translations that they are still taken into account today when scholars seek to establish critical editions of the Greek text of Aristotle.

We must not regard the influx of Aristotle as purely a happy expansion of literary resources. The world view conveyed by the Aristotelian treatises could easily be regarded as a rival of the Christian universe itself as this had been described by the great Fathers of the Church and by their medieval successors. Although by doing so we run the risk of seeming to minimize the vertiginous dimensions of the cultural clash, we can indicate the nature of the supposed threat by citing three real or apparent Aristotelian tenets which collided, or seemed to collide, with Christian belief. First, there is Aristotle's assumption, in his proof of the Prime Mover, that the realm of mobile being has always been.[3] In a word, Aristotle proceeds as if the world had always existed. But it is a matter of Christian belief, based on Genesis, that the world and time had a beginning. Second, if his Moslem interpreters could be believed, Aristotle, in offering what can

be called a proof of the immortality of the soul by appeal to
the nature of the agent intellect, is not arguing that your soul
or mine survives death, but that a single separate entity, the
Tenth Intelligence, which makes use of particular earthly souls
in order to think, survives their disappearance just as it has
anticipated their coming into being.[4] But surely if my soul
does not survive death, indeed if I myself do not, then the
Christian promises are meaningless. Third, in describing God
as thought thinking itself,[5] Aristotle seems to suggest that for
God's knowledge to depend on anything outside and other than
himself would be demeaning and imperfect. But that in turn
seems to suggest that God does not know and direct what is
happening in the world, and what then of the belief in
providence?

Thomas's approach to these difficulties differed from that of
others, notably that of St. Bonaventure. We shall be turning
in a moment to Thomas's treatment of these three problems,
but first a word on the commentaries he wrote on works of
Aristotle. We pointed out in the previous chapter precisely
which works of Aristotle Thomas commented on; he did not
comment on all the works and not every commentary he started
was brought to completion. What sort of thing was a
commentary?

Very roughly, what are called the commentaries of Thomas
are of two kinds. On the one hand, we find him working from
a text as from a springboard, with his own discussion organized
and conducted in relative freedom from the occasioning text.
For example, in commenting on the Sentences of Peter Lombard
or on the De trinitate of Boethius, Thomas, after giving a preliminary outline of a passage, a divisio textus, goes on to discuss
the issues it raises in a more or less independent way, arranging
and dividing the discussion as suits his own purpose. The
commentaries on Aristotle, on the other hand, like those on
Scripture, are far more closely related to the text which provides the order and treatment of issues. A section of the text is
subjected to a searching and, as it were, interlinear scrutiny
before Thomas passes on to the next section. What is given as
the meaning or sense of the text is thus easily checked against
the passage under interpretation. The old saw that Thomas

baptized Aristotle suggests a most inaccurate picture of what we find when we examine the commentaries on Aristotle. Thomas's contemporaries may be excused for thinking that the influence was going rather in the opposite direction, that Thomas submerged himself not wisely but too well in the task of clarifying the sense of the Aristotelian treatises.

In our time, largely through the influence of Werner Jaeger,[6] it has become customary to regard the treatises of Aristotle as, if not random compilations, nonetheless quite imperfect literary wholes. It can thus come as a shock to read Thomas's commentary on the *Metaphysics* of Aristotle—to take the work that is the test case—and see him patiently explaining the coherence of the work, the reason for the order among the books (Thomas commented on twelve of the fourteen books), and seeing an inexorable progression from book to book, from chapter to chapter, from line to line. When Thomas rejects an earlier interpretation, as often as not it is because the interpreter failed to account for the intrinsic order of the Aristotelian work. What is to be said about this fundamental difference between Thomas's approach to Aristotle and that which is, or was until recently, dominant today? Nothing of a general or sweeping sort, perhaps. The ultimate basis for choosing between them must be the text of which both methods purport to be giving an account. If the detailed coherence and interrelations of an Aristotelian treatise that Thomas invites us to see are in no way provided by what Aristotle wrote, then surely something as remarkable as, if not more remarkable than, baptizing is going on.

The works of Aristotle were proscribed at the University of Paris in 1210 and in 1215.[7] The documents say that the books in question are not to be read (*nec legantur*), but this must be taken in the technical sense as meaning that they were not to form the basis for lectures. Furthermore, the prohibition was local. The University of Toulouse made a point of announcing that works of Aristotle which were not lectured on at Paris were lectured on at Toulouse. It seems tolerably clear that the situation at Paris was due to tension between the Faculty of Arts and the Faculty of Theology, with the former pitting the "new philosophy" of Aristotle against traditional theological figures. However this may be, the prohibitions (and they were to be followed by others, notably that of 1277) suggest caution rather than obscurantism. The concern is not to burn the books of Aristotle or to pretend that they do not exist, but rather, in an unhurried and serious way, to assess their philosophical credentials and the impact that the Aristotelian doctrine might have on Christian faith. It was to this dual task that Thomas Aquinas bent some of his best efforts.

II   *The Eternity of the World*

The short work of Thomas Aquinas entitled *On the Eternity of the World* is directed against those who, accepting on faith that the world did in fact have a beginning in time, concluded that it was thereby inconceivable that the world should not have had a beginning in time.[8] Thomas proposes to investigate the matter and it is important to see what he is and what he is not doing. He is not questioning the truth of faith that the world had a beginning in time. He is not asking if the world could always have existed *independently of the divine causality*. "That is an abominable error, not only from the point of view of faith, but also from the point of view of philosophers, who contend and prove that whatever in any way is can only be insofar as it is caused by one who maximally and most truly is." The question Thomas asks, accordingly, is this: Is it conceivable that something caused by God could always have been?

Since God is omnipotent, all would agree that he could have created such an eternal world, if such a world were possible. On the side of the world, there would seem to be two bases for saying that an eternal world is an impossibility. The first has to do with the way in which something's being made seems to presuppose its potential existence in something prior to it. That is, before the statue comes to be, it is potentially in the marble: the marble can become a statue. Well, Thomas says in reply, consider an angel. Before the angel comes to be, it cannot be said that it, or anything else, can become an angel. There is no presupposed stuff out of which an angel comes to be. Nonetheless, God was able to make an angel, because he did so. So too, Thomas observes, there is no passive potency independent of God such that it could have become the world.

"But from this it does not follow that God could not have made some being which has always been."

A second way in which it might be said that an eternal world is impossible is by claiming that the very notion of such a world is self-contradictory and incoherent, on a par with saying that an affirmation and its denial are simultaneously true. Things that are impossible because they make no sense cannot be caused by God and this is scarcely a restriction on or diminution of his omnipotence. That God cannot bring it about that what is true is also false does not detract from his power. Can God bring it about that the past has not been? Thomas takes it to be false to answer this affirmatively because he regards the question as involving conceptual incoherence. Nevertheless, he adds that those who have maintained that God can cause the past not to have been were not thereby called heretics. He seems to be reminding his unnamed opponents that the charge of heresy should not be bandied about lightly. What Thomas wants to know is whether there is a conceptual incoherence, a logical contradiction, in the claim that God could have created an eternal world. To say that God could have created such a world is not, Thomas underlines, heretical. If there is conceptual incoherence, then of course the claim is false. If there is no conceptual incoherence, then it is true that God could have created such a world and false to deny that he could have. St. Thomas means to show that it is not a contradiction to say that God caused a world which has always existed. If there were a contradiction here, it would follow from two factors, taken singly or in conjunction: (1) an agent cause must precede its effect in duration; and (2) nonbeing must precede being in duration, since the world is said to have been created by God from nothing, *ex nihilo.*

Thomas gives a number of reasons to show that the agent cause, God, need not precede his effect if he has so willed it. We shall not give the tightest argument Thomas offers because it is also the most difficult to grasp without a great deal of explication. It must be said, however, that all four of the arguments proposed rely on a distinction between an agent or making cause which presupposes something passive and an agent cause which does not make this presupposition. For something

to be created is not for it to come to be as the result of a
change, since change implies that something which was not F
comes to be F, as the marble which does not have the shape
of Truman comes to have the shape of Truman due to the
agency of the sculptor. God as creator does not shape a preexistent and independent something into creatures. That being
said, let us consider the second of the four arguments Thomas
gives.

The cause which produces the whole substance of its effect
ought to be able to do at least as much as the causes which
produce a form in a preexistent matter, and indeed a good
deal more. But there are agents which produce form alone and
which are simultaneous with their effect such that whenever
the cause is given, its effect is also given. For example, light
as cause of illumination does not exist prior to illumining.
Therefore, and yet more obviously, it is possible that God,
who produces his effects in their totality, not presupposing any
matter or passive potency, could have effects which are whenever he is. And, since God is eternal, the conclusion is that
God could have effects which are eternal.

Having concluded on the basis of this and three other arguments that there is nothing contradictory in saying that a cause
need not precede its effect in duration, Thomas asks whether,
given the fact that God creates the world from nothing, there
must have been some time when the world was not. Here too
he gives several arguments in favor of the view that God's
effect need not not have been at some time prior to its being
caused. One is taken from St. Anselm and has to do with the
phrase "ex nihilo." Anselm observes that when a man is said
to be sad without cause, we say that nothing saddens him.
So too when the world is said to be made from nothing, the
intent is not to suggest that there is something, nothing with
a capital N, as it were, out of which the world was formed and
which preexisted the world. But it could be taken to mean
that the world comes to be *after* not having been, though not
out of or *from* its not having been. Furthermore, Thomas con-
cedes that it must be said that, for creatures, nothing is prior
to being. But he distinguishes a priority of nature and a priority
of time. That which belongs to a thing in and of itself is

naturally prior to that which it has from outside, as it were. But existence is something that every creature has, not from itself, but from God, such that, considered in itself, without reference to God's causality, the creature is nothing.[9] This priority of nothing over being is one of nature and not one of duration, however. "What is being said is not that, if the creature always was, that at some time it was nothing, but rather that its nature is such that, left to itself, it would be nothing."

Thomas concludes that there is nothing conceptually repugnant in the claim that something has been made by God and yet has always been. If such a claim is contradictory, he adds rhetorically, it is marvelous that St. Augustine did not notice it, since it would have provided the most efficacious way of showing that the world is not eternal. Needless to say, the recognition that an eternal world *could* have been created by God is not an argument for the factual eternity of the world. If the conception of an eternal created world were contradictory, then of course arguments on its behalf would be otiose.

The position of St. Thomas, then, is this. While he firmly accepts as revealed truth, as a truth of faith, that the duration of the world had a beginning, that time and the world began, he does not regard the contradictory of this truth to be self-contradictory and false on that basis. God might have done what he did not in fact do, namely, create an eternal world. Nonetheless, if it is true that the world and time had a beginning, then the contradictory of this is false though meaningful. Since it is false, it could not be shown to be true. But have there not been philosophical arguments on behalf of the eternity of the world? There have been. And notably that of Aristotle. What does Thomas have to say of them? In the *Summa theologiae* he writes:

The arguments Aristotle puts forth are not demonstrative in the strict sense but only broadly speaking, since what they do is disprove those arguments of the ancients which attempted to show that the world has come to be in one of the ways in which this is truly impossible. This is clear from three facts. First, both in the Eighth Book of the *Physics* and in the First Book of *On the Heavens* he

first sets down opinions of Anaxagoras and Empedocles and Plato
against which he then fashions contradictory arguments. Second,
wherever he speaks of this matter, he introduces the testimony of the
ancients, which is not the method of one who demonstrates, but rather
of one who would persuade rhetorically. Third, he expressly speaks
in the First Book of the *Topics* of those dialectical problems which
are unresolvable by argument, among them, whether the world is
eternal.[10]

We shall return in a later chapter to Thomas's views on
the relations between what is believed and what is known
or knowable. The discussion of the eternity of the world suggests perhaps the suppleness of his approach as well as the
complexity of his attitude toward Aristotle. He is clearly
impatient with those who are quick to label their opponents
heretics. He is uncharacteristically ironic in his treatment of
those who assume that the contradictory of a revealed truth
is unthinkable simply because the believer knows it to be
false. Further, because the believer holds that the claim that
the world is eternal is false does not mean that he is thereby
provided with arguments to that effect nor with disproofs of
arguments which purport to show the opposite of what God
has revealed. It is sufficient, incidentally, that such arguments
be shown not to be conclusive. It may well be, as Thomas
seems to have held, that there is no conclusive argument for
the proposition that the world and time had a beginning.

A final word. When the world is said to be eternal, this
term cannot be understood in the same sense it has when
God is said to be eternal.[11] Endless duration on the part of
that which is susceptible to change and alteration is unlike
the divine duration, since God's eternity is total and simultaneous possession of the summation of perfection.

III   *The Nature of Man*

If man is a moral agent with a destiny that extends beyond
this life, he is nonetheless one among the variety of natural
beings. Indeed, when Thomas speaks of the characteristics of
man that set him apart from other natural creatures and enable

him to transcend the cosmos, he makes use of a vocabulary first fashioned to talk of physical objects. In this, he is following Aristotle for whom "soul" is a term that ranges over a spectrum including mice and men, foliage and fish. Moreover, as we shall see, soul is a special case of that constituent or element of physical things that makes them to be what they are. To say that man is composed of body and soul is a special way of saying that he is composed of matter and form. Thomas takes over from Aristotle the view that the physical thing, that is, whatever has come to be as a result of a change, is composed of matter and form.

A. The Structure of Physical Objects

So pervasive is this analysis of the structure of physical objects in the thought of Thomas that it may seem to be merely a technical jargon derived from Aristotle. If this were all it was, we could learn it as we do any odd or coded use of language, and that would be that. Far more interesting, of course, would be to see what arguments and analyses this use of language depends upon. As it happens, Thomas on many occasions justifies this way of talking about physical things and it is quite clear that for him that justification resides in the way things are and not simply in the conventions of language. In commenting on the *Physics* of Aristotle,[12] Thomas gives a masterly explication of the key classical text and, in an independent short work, *On the Principles of Nature*,[13] he argues for the truth of the claim that physical things, products of natural change, are made up of two factors, matter (*hyle*) and form (*morphe*). Because of the Greek terminology, this is often called the hylomorphic theory.

The Latin term *natura*, like its Greek counterpart *physis*, suggests the process of being born, of coming to be.[14] Thus, it is not surprising that by *nature* is meant the realm of change, of alteration, of coming to be and passing away, and by *natural things* those which have come to be as a result of a change, which alter and move constantly while they are, and ultimately undergo a change that terminates their being. The terms *universum* and *cosmos* suggest order, but if the natural world has order and structure, this is not so much static as dynamic and conative.[15]

The hylomorphic theory is formulated as an answer to the question: What can we say of anything whatsoever that has come to be as the result of a change? That is, this is the first and not the last analysis; it is the least that can be said of natural things since, if accurate, it applies to them all, whatever may be their differences. This is not to say that it is explicitly based on anything like a tour of the cosmos. Rather, taking any homely instance of change as typical, an analysis is offered which purports to be a generalization of the kind mentioned. Nor should we wonder that the examples tend to be drawn from human affairs.

Consider the child who learns the multiplication table and whose proud parents say, "Junior has become a mathematician." This would not be an appropriate remark when the multiplication table is recited by someone who has long known it. Junior, from not knowing the multiplication table, has come to know it. Let us, following Aristotle and St. Thomas, observe that this change can be expressed in a number of ways:

(1)   A human being becomes educated.
(2)   The uneducated becomes educated.
(3)   The uneducated human being becomes educated.

Each expression of the change listed here has the structure, "X becomes Y."[16] What expressions could be altered to the equally familiar structure, "From X, Y comes to be"? If the latter locution suggests, as it seems to, that X ceases to be when Y comes to be, then (1) would not be expressible in this fashion, though both (2) and (3) would be.

(2′)   From the uneducated, the educated comes to be.
(3′)   From the uneducated human being, the educated comes to be.

This in turn suggests that the grammatical subjects of (2) and (3) do not stand for, do not signify, the subject of the change, that to which the change is attributed, that which survives the change. We want to say that the man who was not educated has come to be educated. That is, a minimal account of any change would have to cite that which changes, the subject of the change, as well as the new determination or designation it takes on as a result of the change. Furthermore, the subject must not have had, must have been deprived of, that determination or designation before the change occurs. These elements of change receive as quasi-technical names: matter (subject, *hyle*), form (determination, shape, *morphe*), and privation (the not having, the privation, the *steresis* of a form the subject is capable of having). Against this background we can see why it is said that the result of a change is a compound of matter and form, that is, in our example, of human being and educated.

This account is meant to apply to a variety of changes, as for example to an object's moving from place to place, to its taking on new qualities such as temperature and color, and to its increase and decrease in quantity, as in gaining weight or losing it. In changes of this kind, the subject becomes such-and-such as a result of the change, that is, it comes to be here as opposed to there, to be tan as opposed to pale, to be tall as opposed to short, but the subject itself does not come to be as such or without qualification. Junior may become a mathematician as a result of learning the multiplication tables, but he does not come to be absolutely speaking or without qualification. As we have seen, the subject of the change is presupposed by it and survives it. Changes in place, in quality, in quantity are therefore called accidental changes, in the sense that by them the subject comes to be only in a certain respect. The question must then arise: Can substances themselves be regarded as unqualified terms of change?

No more than Aristotle would Thomas presume to *prove* that there is such a thing as substantial change, that is, a change whose term is a substance and not merely a new condition or accident of a preexisting substance. Rather, he would ask: Are there obvious macrocosmic things which exist in their own right, which are things and not merely aspects or accidents of things? An affirmative answer to this question is based on the belief that Socrates, a horse, or a tree are autonomous beings or substances. Have such things come to be? Will they cease to be? Clearly, these questions must be answered in the affirmative. Of what help can the preceding analysis of change be in explaining such substantial changes?

The matter or subject involved in accidental change is itself

a substance. If the matter of a substantial change were in turn
a substance, then any form acquired by the change would
relate to that substance as an accidental form, and then the
change would be an accidental and not a substantial one. If
substantial change is change, it requires a subject, and if it
is substantial change, its subject cannot be itself a substance.
It was to get at this feature of substantial change that the
term "prime matter" was devised. The form that prime matter
takes on, since it is constitutive of a substance and not merely
of a new state of a substance, is called substantial form. Thus,
by analogy with the principles of accidental change,[17] we can
speak of the principles of substantial change. It is on this basis
that Thomas will say that physical or natural substances, substances that have come to be as the result of a change, are
composed of form and matter.

B. The Structure of Man

It can now be seen what Thomas means by saying that man
is composed of soul and body. Like other physical substances,
he has come to be and is thus a compound of form and matter.
Soul is the name for the substantial form of living things.
Aristotle defines the soul as the first act, that is, the substantial
form, of an organic body.[18] He goes on to say that soul is that
whereby we first move, live, sense, and understand. These
two descriptions of soul move from the generic to the specific.
The first definition is applicable to the substantial form of
any living thing, though its applicability to man and animal is
most obvious. The second definition, by making explicit use of
the personal pronoun, is clearly meant as a statement about
the human soul. Thomas accepts the Aristotelian doctrine of
types or kinds of soul which are denominated from the highest
capacity or faculty they give rise to. On this basis, there is a
vegetative, sensitive, and intellectual soul. Furthermore, there
is a telescoping effect, as it were, such that the sensitive or
animal soul possesses the vegetative powers and more besides,
and the intellectual soul possesses the powers of the vegetative
and sensitive soul and more besides.[19] That "more besides" in
the case of the human soul is of course intellect or reason.

This is not to say that man has three souls. This cannot be the case because of what has already been said about the nature of substantial change. If the intellectual soul came as a modification to an already existing living thing that survived the change, the intellectual soul would have to be an accident and would not be constitutive of what man is essentially. Indeed, to be a man would not on this supposition be an essential designation.

Our discussion must, of course, be a limited one. We wish to concentrate on the human soul and to do so according to the following plan. Since the human soul is designated from intellection, as from the highest capacity it gives rise to, we must say something about Thomas's understanding of mind, of knowledge. This has particular importance because it is by appeal to the nature of intellection that both Thomas and Aristotle argue for the continued existence of the human soul after death. This conception of the immortality of the soul gives rise to two problems that must be faced. It is perhaps clear from our presentation of the concepts of substantial form and prime matter that these are constituent parts of substances and not substances in their own right. What is not a substance in its own right cannot, by definition, enjoy an autonomous existence. How then within the confines of his Aristotelianism can Thomas claim that the soul survives death? To this problem must be conjoined the issue as to whether or not Aristotle himself held to the soul's survival. Many of Thomas's contemporaries thought not. Thomas, in the opusculum *On the Unicity of the Intellect*[20] says yes. Further, how can this argument for the survival of the human soul be squared with the Christian belief in the resurrection? The Christian puts his hope in a personal immortality. But a man's soul is not man. *Anima mea non sum ego*, as Thomas himself wrote: I am not my soul. We must ask how Thomas reconciles the Aristotelian argument, as he reads it, and the Christian belief.

1. Cognition and the Cosmos

In the *Disputed Question on Truth*,[21] Thomas provides us with a panoramic view of the universe and of the place of the knowing or cognitive being in it. The passage is remarkable for the way in which it exhibits the extension of the matter-form analysis from the physical or entitative order to the cognitive or intentional order. Just as in physical becoming a subject takes on a form, so too in coming to know, Thomas suggests, the knower takes on the form of other things.

A thing can be said to be perfected or completed in two ways, the first of which, call it entitative perfection, derives, at least in natural things, from substantial form. The natural thing is constituted or is thanks to the actualizing of matter by form. Thanks to this, it has a specific sort of being. It is possible in a not wholly Pickwickian way to regard this perfection as a limitation or imperfection. That is to say, if each thing has the specific perfection it has, it is thereby distinguished from things which have other sorts of perfection that it does not itself have. To be is to be a kind of thing, and to be a thing of a particular kind is not to be in the vast variety of ways that specifically other things are. Entitative perfection results in a kind of segregation and isolation. A thing is what it is and not another thing. Thus, the perfection of anything is a limited perfection distinguishing it from all other sorts of perfection, a part of the total perfection of the universe. Into this picture of things, knowledge is introduced as a remedy for the isolation and differences among things.

That there might be a remedy for such imperfection another mode of perfection is found among created things whereby the perfection which is proper to one thing can be found in another. This is the perfection of the knower insofar as he is a knower, for what is known by the knower is in some way in the knower. That is why it is said, in the Third Book of *On the Soul*, that the soul is in a certain manner all things, because it is fashioned to know all things.[22]

Thanks to knowledge, the perfection of the whole universe can be present to or in one thing. The ultimate perfection to which the soul can aspire, philosophers maintained, was to have the whole order of the universe inscribed within it. They identified man's ultimate end with this condition, and do we not, asks Thomas, ourselves see man's ultimate end as the vision of God? And, with St. Gregory, Thomas asks what would not be seen by those who see God?

Needless to say, it is not immediately clear what could be meant by saying that the perfection of one thing is had by another. Surely this could not be in the same way that the perfection or substantial form determines the other thing by making it what it is, the kind of thing it is. Knowledge does not make the knower a specifically different entity from what he was before knowing. We must, then, find a way in which the perfection of another is had in knowing and which will differ from the way that perfection makes the other thing what it is.

Thomas observes that the forms and perfections of things are received in matter: that is how a substance of a specific kind is constituted. The first requirement will be that the form or perfection is received otherwise than it is received by matter, and thus the thing will be knowable insofar as it is separated from matter. This in turn entails that that which receives the perfection of another thing be immaterial. If it were material, the perfection would be received in it as it is received in matter and the result would be another thing of that kind. When prime matter is the subject of substantial form, the result is a specific kind of substance. If substantial form is to be received in a subject in such a way that the result is not a substantial change, the production of a new substance, the subject cannot be the kind of subject that matter is. But if it is not a subject like matter, it is an immaterial subject and the form or perfection is said to be received or had or possessed in an immaterial way. A lion considered as a natural substance is a compound of matter and form. To know a lion, to know what a lion is, is to have that which makes a lion the kind of thing it is, namely, its form. But to possess what-it-is-to-be-a-lion in the cognitive way is not thereby to become another lion, to undergo a substantial change. The latter sort of change results in a new individual; possession of the form in knowledge is to have that which represents each and every instance of it. No doubt my concept of lion is something singular, one among many concepts I have, but its content is such that it does not represent this lion as opposed to that but rather what-it-is-to-be-a-lion, the perfection of leoninity. For the form to be had without material conditions, principal among which is individuation, is for it to be had in a universal way: to be some one thing which is common to many.[23] We will have something more to say in a moment about the way in which intellection is said to be an immaterial activity.

This sketch of the universe and of man's place in it suggests that while he is one sort of thing among many others, the totality of perfection can nonetheless be inscribed in his soul. Man as microcosm can thus be understood in several ways. In one sense, what he is includes the perfections of lesser things and more besides. The characteristics of inorganic things as well as of lower forms of life are found in him. Thus, in an entitative way, man may be said to sum up the cosmos. And, of course, the isolation of things which cannot know does not preclude interaction and order which result from such relations as cause and effect. What Thomas is after is that special sort of relation where the knower is aware of, has present to him as other, the perfections of specifically different things. Indeed, for man to know what he himself is is to have his entitative perfection in an intentional way. This intentional presence or possession of the perfections of all other things makes man a microcosm, the universe writ small, as it were, in a special way.

Needless to say, the account here given of knowledge is not meant to explain every sense of knowing. What Thomas is sketching is the way in which concepts of things are had by the knower, but this kind of knowing, he feels, is presupposed by other kinds such as knowing that something is the case, that it is implied by other things that are the case, or knowing how to do or perform a given activity.

2. Intellect and Survival After Death

We are now in a position to consider the controverted question as to what exactly Aristotle's teaching on the status of intellect was. Among the Arabic commentators, Averroes, as well as his followers in the West, the so-called Latin Averroists, took Aristotle to be saying that, since the activity of intellect is immaterial, it enjoys a separate existence, separate from this human soul or that. In short, it had the status of an immaterial entity, like that of an angel, rather than the status of a capacity or faculty that each man has because of the kind of soul he has. This seemingly *recherché* textual point has an importance it is well to underline. As we shall be suggesting, Aristotle's proof that the soul can exist after death is based upon the fact that the activity of intellect is an immaterial one. But if intellect is not a faculty of my soul, this will not provide an argument for the continued existence of *my* soul after death. Rather, as the Averroists claim, all Aristotle has shown is that intellect, which is not a faculty of my soul, enjoys an existence independent of matter and thus its existence is unaffected by the death of this man or that. If that were the case and if no other argument for the continued existence of this human soul or that could be found, there would be no basis other than faith on which to maintain that a man is destined for an unending existence beyond this earthly life. Moreover, if it were maintained, as apparently some medievals did maintain, that, from a philosophical point of view, we *know* the soul does not survive death, then the belief that it does so survive would entail a contradiction.

That some believers professed not to find such a conflict between knowledge and belief repugnant was unintelligible to Thomas Aquinas. The tack he takes here is of utmost importance. He argues at great length, in the first chapter of *On the Unicity of the Intellect*,[24] that Averroes and his followers are wrong on historical and textual grounds in interpreting Aristotle as they do. His argument is that the writings of Aristotle, particularly *On the Soul*, make it clear that the great Greek philosopher holds that while the human soul is the first act or substantial form of body, and while the intellect is a faculty or capacity of the human soul, nonetheless the activity of the intellect, understanding, is not a vital act that involves a corporeal organ. Thus, the intellect is separate in several senses: it is a separate faculty of the soul, differing from its other faculties, and its activity is separate from matter in the sense of being immaterial. Thomas argues that this is not to say that intellect is something existing separately from the soul, although it does provide the basis for saying that the soul which has such a faculty is capable of existence independently of or separately from the body. That is, the human soul, man's substantial form, unlike the substantial forms of all other natural substances, does not exist simply as a result of its composition with matter; rather it has existence and confers existence on the body. This is not to say, however, that the soul exists prior to man.

The polemical opusculum that Thomas directed against the Averroists is of fundamental importance in deciding the nature and quality of the Aristotelianism of Thomas Aquinas. Written before his commentary on *On the Soul*,[25] it is explicit in what it set out to do, namely, to show that the text of Aristotle does not permit the Averroistic interpretation. There can be no doubt that Thomas is loath to think that so great a thinker as Aristotle should have taught something on so basic a point that would conflict with revealed truth. But the source of this attitude must be found in his knowledge of the text of Aristotle, not in some rhetorical urge to gild the truths of faith by showing their concordance with Aristotelian doctrine. However, the matter need not and should not be discussed at such a speculative level. We have the exegetical account of Aristotle's doctrine offered by Thomas and that must be assessed, not with reference to his motives, wishes, or hopes, but rather with reference to the Aristotelian text in question. Does Thomas's account of what Aristotle taught square with what Aristotle wrote? That it is a far more tenable and defensible interpretation than that offered by Averroes on the point in question here would seem to be beyond doubt.

It is difficult to go beyond the point we have now reached without introducing matters which would invite us to go yet further into the niceties of what Thomas taught concerning the human soul. We have, in the foregoing, mentioned without explaining it the notion of faculties or capacities of the human soul. Nor have we even alluded to a problem that will have occurred to the reader. If the possession of the form of another in cognition is immaterial and thus grounds for an argument showing the possible continued existence of the soul of the knower after death, does this not entail as well the immortality of the animal soul, since, for Thomas, perception or sensing is a kind of knowledge? It will have to suffice here to assert that Thomas offers arguments on behalf of the notion of faculties of the soul, and on behalf of a distinctive difference between sensation and intellection on the question of immaterial reception or possession of forms.[26]

3. Resurrection of the Body

We shall conclude this section by returning to a problem mentioned earlier. Thomas accepts as Aristotelian, and as sound, an argument which concludes that the human soul continues to exist after the death of the human person. If this is called an argument for the immortality or incorruptibility of the human soul, as it is, this does not seem to be the kind of immortality that is involved in Christian belief. The believer hopes for a future personal existence and, as Thomas himself insists, the human person is not simply soul but soul incarnate, body and soul.

For Thomas, death is a punishment consequent upon Original Sin, and our redemption as effected by Christ is, among other things, to repair this damage. Christ's resurrection is symbolic of our destiny and, as St. Paul observed, if Christ did not rise from the dead, then our hope is in vain. At the end of time, the Christian believes, there will be a general resurrection and the beginning of an unending personal life, not merely as a separate soul but as body and soul.[27] Needless to say, Thomas does not imagine that Aristotle had any intimation of immortality in this sense. Indeed, he excuses Aristotle for not speculating on the nature of the separate existence of the soul, apart from the body.[28] That man is destined for a future life of immortality which, so to speak, cancels mortality at its root and redeems the separation of soul and body in death could not have been known by man apart from its being announced by God himself. We have here, perhaps, another instance of the misleading character of the claim that Thomas baptizes Aristotle. The "baptized" conception of immortality is not one that Thomas would dream of ascribing to Aristotle. Indeed, as we have suggested, Thomas's plea for a textually justifiable interpretation of Aristotle's teaching on the human soul and the human intellect is just that. To speak of it somehow as a determined effort to make Aristotle say what Christians believe is simply to overlook the true dimensions of the Christian belief in personal immortality. To say that what Aristotle taught does not contradict the latter is far from claiming that the pagan philosopher had any intimation of what God has prepared for those who love him.

IV   Man as Moral Agent

"As Damascene says," Thomas writes, "man is said to be made to the image of God insofar as by image is meant intellectual, free in judgment and capable of autonomous action. Thus, after the discussion of the Exemplar, that is, of God, and of those things which his power voluntarily produces according to his image, we now go on to discuss his image, that is, man, insofar as he is the principle of his own activity because he has free will and the power over his own deeds."[29]

This is the Prologue to the Second Part of the *Summa theologiae*, the so-called moral part of that great work. In the First Part of the *Summa*, as the passage quoted suggests, Thomas considered the nature and attributes of God, the Trinity of Persons in God, and then creation. That part of the *Summa* draws to a close with the famous Treatise on Man,[30] passages of which we have been relying on in our discussion of Thomas's views on the soul. With respect to creatures higher than man, the angels, purely spiritual creatures, their eternal destiny is already settled by a decisive choice between good and evil. The good angels are those who have chosen God's plan, the bad angels, or devils, those who out of pride asserted their own will against God's. It is because such creatures act with a lucidity that is considered to exceed to an unimaginable degree any that we might summon that a single choice sufficed to settle their eternal status.[31] With respect to creatures less than man, the vast range of nonliving things and the spectrum through the life-world from the simplest living substance to the higher animals whose senses and perception in some ways rival and surpass man's own, there does not seem to be a moral task imposed. True, in Thomas's view, such things are so constituted that they pursue goals, their activity can be seen as purposive, but unlike man they are said not to direct themselves to an end. That is, they do not propose alternative ends to themselves, select from among them, and direct themselves to the chosen goal.[32] Of course Thomas does not think that all subhuman creatures are alike in their activity. If it is true that none of them is self-directive, in the sense we have yet to clarify, it is also true that as one moves up the scale from the inorganic into the life-world and through the various ranks within it, there is an increase of indetermination in the activity of things, a growth of spontaneity. This is a point worth dwelling on.

A. Man and Nature

In commenting on Aristotle's *On the Soul,* Thomas invokes a distinction between the natural world and the life-world.[33] Now, as we have previously seen, the realm of nature is originally viewed as including all spatio-temporal things, whatever has come to be as a result of a change. Physical objects, as they are first discussed, are not distinguished from living substances. Thus, when Thomas makes a distinction within the natural or physical world between the natural and the vital, he is using "natural" in a more restricted sense. And the distinction is one that is employed not simply to distinguish one kind of substance from another, but to speak of different aspects of living substance. That is, the living substance not only has features which lead us to distinguish it from the nonliving; it also shares features with nonliving things. It is these shared and thus more common features which come to be called natural in order to distinguish them from the distinctive features or characteristics of the living. Furthermore, on this basis, Thomas will speak of nature as determined to one effect, to one end. This determination to one, *determinatio ad unum,*[34] may be thought of in terms of the negation, E and not-E. The more natural a thing is, the more likely it is that it will be determined to its end or function or operation, E, in such a way that not-E is simply excluded. Consider the somewhat curious doctrine of natural place. The elements—fire, air, earth, and water—are taken to have natural places in the cosmos such that it is their nature to move toward them. Fire, for example, flies up, earth descends. It is as if each is determined by its nature to that end or place. Complex things are not thus determined with regard to the goal of their locomotion, but we would no doubt want to hold that there is a finite number of activities which could be ascribed to a given entity as that given entity. Imagine, for example, that the properties associated with iron make up a finite list, and so too with the properties of marble. We just do not expect any and every activity to be associated with a given substance like iron. When we move into the world of life, the variety and indeterminancy increase. In the case of locomotion, Thomas offers the simple example of a plant. Its growth involves pushing itself up and down and out in every direction. With the advent of sense perception, the possibilities of activity multiply and it becomes progressively more difficult to exhaust the variety of deeds that might naturally be associated with an animal.

This background is useful when we turn to Thomas's way of distinguishing man from all other natural creatures. It would be quite wrong to think that he sees the cosmos as a programmed and determined place where each thing is being guided along a predestined path in very much the same way. For Thomas, there is a real indeterminancy in the natural world and it increases as we move upward toward man. Moreover, this increase in indeterminancy is a function of the increasing self-determination of creatures of higher sorts. The plant is a center and source of agency in a way that a mineral is not; the animal is to a far greater extent than the plant the originator of its natural history; and, again, there are degrees within the animal kingdom. Thus, when Thomas turns to man as the image of God because he has free will and is the master of his own activity, he clearly means to cite a qualitative difference, but it is a difference that is added to what is also found in the subhuman viewed as encompassing a vast declension down through a scale of progressively less self-determination toward the fully natural, that is, things that are determined to one and only one end.[35]

It is all but impossible for us to speak of such things without employing locutions suggestive of evolution. Lest any misunderstanding arise, it should be said that Thomas nowhere speaks of man as emerging from a vast prehistory of development, from the simpler forms of life. When he compares man and other living things, he insists on structural similarities. To speak of growth and sensation and sense desire as things found in plants, beasts, and man is not, for Thomas, to speak metaphorically. He holds that there are univocal meanings of these terms which permit them to encompass animals and plants and men. That is why he can think of man as the creature in whom are summed up all levels of being found in things less than himself, but with the addition of the determining or defining features of the human.[36] Man as microcosm. He can be weighed like iron, he grows like a plant, he moves himself about, he perceives, he wants or shuns what he perceives as do animals. But beyond all these shared features, he has other characteristics which lead us to see him as a distinct species. What we have then is, as it were, a static rather than a dynamic panorama of the relations among material creatures. We can imagine, as Thomas himself did,[37] the figures of plane geometry— the triangle, the square, the various polygons—in such a way that the earlier items on the list are included in the latter, a kind of Chinese box in which these figures nest. That is what we mean by a static view. Opposed to it would be the dynamic view, according to which the more complex figures would emerge out of the simpler and function, so to speak, as the dialectical limit of them.

If Thomas did not hold anything like an evolutionary view, there is nonetheless a curious claim not unlike "ontogeny recapitulates phylogeny" in remarks he makes about the human fetus. He seems to distinguish in the period of gestation between a plant stage, an animal stage, and a fully human stage, when the soul is infused by God. This has tempted many interpreters as a possible opening toward the evolutionary. Perhaps. But that evolution can be argued to be *compatible* with positions Thomas did in fact hold is very far from providing a basis for the claim that he actually adumbrated the evolutionary theory.

B. Free Will

What now of the distinctive characteristic that leads to man's being called the image of God? That characteristic is free will, or, as Thomas prefers to call it, free judgment, *liberum arbitrium*.[38] What we find in Thomas is not so much a proof or argument to the effect that man is free as an account or analysis of what it is for him to be free. It is true that he often suggests a *reductio ad absurdum* of the denial of human freedom. If man is not free, then deliberation, advice, precepts, prohibitions, rewards, and punishments are pointless.[39] Which means, among other things, that he who would deny that man is free must provide some account of the kinds of activities just mentioned. Given that man is free, we need an account of his freedom. The following is a typical argument from the several to be found in the writings of Thomas.

For a clarification of this, consider that some beings act without judgment, as the rock moves downward, and similarly all things which lack knowledge. Other things act with judgment indeed, but not with free judgment, like brute animals. For the sheep seeing the wolf judges that she should flee by a natural judgment which is not free since it does not involve pondering (*non ex collatione*), but she judges by natural instinct. So it is with every judgment of the brute animal. Now man acts by means of judgment, because through a knowing power he judges that something should be pursued or avoided, yet this judgment is not by a natural instinct toward a particular action but from a rational pondering (*collatione*). Thus he acts by free judgment since he is capable of directing himself in diverse ways. Reason is not bound in contingent matters (that is, obliged to assent to a proposition and reject its contradictory), as is clear from dialectical syllogisms and rhetorical persuasions. Particular things to be done are instances of contingent things and reason is thus open to diverse judgments and not determined to one. For this reason, that man acts from free judgment follows necessarily from the fact that he is rational.[40]

Insofar as reason reveals that there is no single course of action open to us given our ends or goals, we are free with respect to choosing the means. When we act, we are not determined by the way things are, as if only one course were open to us; rather, we determine ourselves as to whether or not we shall act and, if we do, whether we will do this or that. Reason is thus the *radix libertatis*, the root of liberty. We will consider another analysis Thomas gives of human freedom after we have looked at what he has to say of ultimate end.

Turning now to Thomas's moral teaching, we shall take up the following points: that human action is for an end; that there is an ultimate end of human action; that God is man's ultimate end; the relation of freedom and ultimate end;[41] the practical syllogism and natural law. This is a considerable menu, of course, but with effort we should be able to provide both an historically accurate account of what Thomas taught on these matters and one that suggests the plausibility of the positions he adopted. It goes without saying that all these are matters of continuing controversy in moral philosophy and that we do not here pretend to develop the Thomistic teaching in the light of all revelant objections to it.

C. The Teleology of Human Acts

Here, in close paraphrase, is Thomas's argument to the effect that it is peculiar to man as man that he act for an end. Of the various actions men perform, those are properly called human which are peculiar to man as man. But man differs from irrational creatures in this, that he has dominion over his acts. Hence only those acts are properly called human of which man has the dominion. Now man has dominion over his acts thanks to reason and will. Therefore, those actions are properly called human which are due to deliberate will. Whatever other actions pertain to man can be called acts of man but not human acts. Now actions due to a given power are caused by it under the formality of its object. But the object of will is the end and good. Hence it is necessary that human actions as such be for an end.[42]

The elegantly formal procedure is typical of Thomas. Each sentence functions as premise or conclusion in the cumulative argument. Indeed, simply by numbering the sentences, we can make the shape of the proof crystal-clear. It is then an easy matter to test the procedure for its crucial moves and to isolate the premises that require elucidation before they can be accepted or rejected.

(1) Human acts are those proper to man as man.

(2) Man differs from irrational creatures in that he has dominion over his acts.

(3) Only those acts are properly human of which man has dominion.

In (2), the distinguishing characteristic of man, that which sets him apart from other animals, is said to be that he has dominion over his acts. What is said of man in terms of that which he has in common with other animals is not said of him as man; what is said of him in terms of that which is proper or peculiar to him, distinguishing him from other animals, is said of him just insofar as he is a man.

The next step of the argument calls into play the account of free will we have already seen, from which it is concluded that properly human acts stem from deliberate volition. Thomas then distinguishes *acts of man* from *human acts,* a distinction already implicit in the first stage of the argument.[43] Whatever activities can be truly ascribed to man but which are nonetheless shared or common because they do not belong to him properly, exclusively, are not human acts in the sense being developed. For example, activities such as growing, digesting, seeing, aching, and so forth may be truly said of a man, but not as man. First, such activities are not exclusive or peculiar to him; second, they are not due to what is definitive in man, they are not the result of deliberate volition.

The final step of the argument relies on the notion of the formal object of a power or potency. Sight and hearing are not distinguished from one another in that sight bears on, say, trees, elephants, and stars, while hearing is concerned with birds, bushes, and zebras. Something is an object of sight under the formality of color; something is an object of hearing under the formality of sound. The will is a power whose object is the end and good. A thing is called good to the degree that it is an object of desire, of appetency. And of course something is desired insofar as it is regarded as perfective of the desirer. The will, as rational appetite, is the tendency toward whatever reason judges to be perfective of man. From a material point of view, the things that are the objects of will are innumerable: ice cream, justice, comfort, victory, money, and so on. But this is like mentioning, as the object of sight, trees, elephants, and stars. Just as they are visible insofar as they are colored, so things are the object of will insofar as they are good and endlike. Once this somewhat difficult point is grasped, the argument concludes easily: human acts as such are for the sake of the good or end.

That human actions as such are to some end or purpose is not perhaps too surprising a contention. Of any human action whatsoever it is true that it is for some end or purpose. But this of course allows for a quasi-infinity of particular objectives. Thomas wants to maintain not simply that every action has an end but also that there is an ultimate common end or purpose of every action. This is the conception of the ultimate end. It is easily one of the more controversial elements in Thomas's moral teaching, although the concept of ultimate end did not originate with him. The notion of a comprehensive human good which is the ultimate objective of any particular act is, indeed, a familiar one. Nonetheless, it is a hard notion to grasp, not least because one way of illustrating it invites misunderstanding.

The notion of ultimate end is contrasted with that of a proximate end, and the latter may be illustrated by invoking a chain of objectives. For example, a man studies in order to learn biology, he wants to know biology in order to obtain a degree, he wants a degree in order to gain entrance to medical school, he wants to go to medical school in order to become a physician, and he wants to be a doctor in order to heal the sick. What comes last in the list is the ultimate aim of the chain. When now we are told of a single ultimate end of all human activities, we are likely to imagine that there is one objective or aim which shows up on a list with others but which takes precedence over the rest of them. It seems clear that this is not at all what Thomas meant by the ultimate end. This can best be seen when we look at the arguments he fashioned against the suggestion that a man might have a plurality of ultimate ends.

(1) When anything desires its perfection, it desires it as an ultimate end, that is, as its perfect and completing good.

(2) It is thus necessary that the ultimate end so fulfill the

whole appetite of man that nothing outside it remains
to be desired.

(3) It cannot be that there should be two things toward
which appetite could tend as wholly fulfilling of it.[44]

The thing to notice here is the description of ultimate end
that functions in the argument. What is involved is that which
is completely fulfilling and perfective of man. Now, another
way of putting that would be: goodness as such. Consider this
second argument against a plurality of ultimate ends for man.

(4) In the process of rational appetition, there must be
a principle that is naturally desired.

(5) The principle of the process of rational appetite is
ultimate end.

(6) Hence it is necessary that whatever is desired under
the formality of the ultimate end is one.[45]

The ultimate end, it becomes clear, is the formality under
which whatever is chosen is chosen; it is the conception of
that which is fully and completely perfective of the kind of
agent we are. When we see that "happiness" is another word
for "ultimate end," it becomes clear that we are not speaking
of a particular aim or purpose or goal among other particular
ones: we are speaking of the formality under which any
particular goal is pursued.

Of course, to say that a man pursues whatever he pursues
for the sake of his total fulfillment or happiness is platitudinous.
We must go on to ask in what human happiness consists. In
this regard, Thomas distinguishes between an imperfect happiness, that which is attainable in this life, and perfect happiness,
our ultimate destiny. If human action is distinctive because it
is rational, the perfection of rational activity, the virtues perfective of our distinctive kind of activity in its various modes,
will constitute our happiness. Echoing Aristotle,[46] Thomas can
thus offer as a first account of human happiness that it is a
life lived according to virtue. Virtues are perfective of the
activity of reason itself as well as of the rational activity involved
in choice and action. Behind this observation lies the distinction
between the theoretical and practical uses of mind, a distinction
we shall examine in the next chapter. Suffice it to say for now
that while reason has been introduced into the discussion of

morality as a component of deliberate choice, St. Thomas considers that use of reason which has for its end or good the contemplation of truth as the most perfect expression of the distinctive human activity. "And therefore the ultimate and perfect happiness which is expected in the future life will consist wholly in contemplation. That imperfect happiness, however, which can be had here, consists first and primarily of contemplation and secondarily of the operation of the practical intellect ordering human actions and passions, as is said in the Tenth Book of the *Nicomachean Ethics*."[47]

We are now in a position to see why St. Thomas identifies man's ultimate and perfect happiness with the contemplation of God. This can be put most briefly thus. Whatever good, whatever sum of goods, we may pursue and achieve in this life remains incorrigibly particular and partial. No good is goodness itself. Thus, we may say, our appetite for goodness remains forever unassuaged by particular goods, none of which exhausts the formality under which it is pursued, namely, that which is fully and perfectly satisfying of our will. The same point can be made from the side of truth. Whatever the mind grasps, it grasps under the formality of being. But any being we know is a particular being, this one, not being or beingness itself. Some indirect and imperfect knowledge of God, who *is* being, can be achieved in this life by inference and analogy from created effects. But this knowledge can never attain to knowledge of the divine nature, of what God is. "If then the human intellect, knowing the essence of a given effect, knows of God only that he is, it has not yet attained the first cause absolutely speaking, and there remains in it a natural desire to seek knowledge of that cause. Hence it is not yet perfectly happy. For perfect happiness, therefore, the mind must grasp the very essence of the first cause. Thus its perfection will be had in union with God as its object, in whom alone the happiness of man consists."[48] God is not merely another good to be pursued; he is the good that is identical with goodness itself, the fullness of goodness.

This enables Thomas to fashion another account of man's freedom in choice.

Notice that man does not choose necessarily. The reason is that what is such that it can be or not be is not such that it necessarily is. That it is possible to choose or not to choose can be shown in two ways with reference to man's capacity. Man can will or not will, act or not act; and he can will this or will that, do this or do that. This follows from the very power of reason itself. Whatever the reason can apprehend as good, the will can tend toward. Reason can apprehend as good not only to will or to do, but also not to will and not to do. Furthermore, in any particular good can be found both good and the defect of good, that is, evil. Any such good can thus be apprehended as chooseable or as something to be shunned. Only the perfect good which is happiness cannot be regarded by reason as in some way defective. Therefore man wills happiness necessarily; he cannot want to be miserable or unhappy. Choice, however, bearing as it does, not on the end, but on means to the end, is not of the perfect good which is happiness but of other particular goods, and these man chooses not out of necessity but freely.[49]

D.   Theoretical and Practical Thinking

In order to speak of the practical syllogism, we must first consider the distinction Thomas makes between the theoretical, or speculative, use of mind and the practical use of mind, although our emphasis here will be on practical reason. In the following chapter, when we discuss the divisions of the speculative sciences, we will need to go much further into the matter of the theoretical and the practical.

By now the reader will no longer be surprised to find that the textual setting in which a distinction is made and the distinction itself are often surprisingly unrelated, at least at first view. More often than not, the setting is overtly theological and the distinction that interests us is made or recalled in order to be put to some extremely arcane use. Thus it is that one of the best passages in which Thomas discusses human practical knowledge and its degrees occurs when he asks whether God has theoretical or practical knowledge of creatures.[50] We are not concerned with that further theological employment of it but only with the distinction between theoretical and practical knowing.

Stated in its simplest terms, the distinction comes down to this. The theoretical use of our mind aims at the perfection of the knowing process, of knowledge as such, and that perfection is, of course, truth. When our aim is truth, when what we are after is to bring into accord our thinking and the way things are, we are using our minds in a theoretical way. When, on the other hand, we make use of our minds not chiefly to attain the perfection of thinking as such but rather the perfection of some activity other than thinking, for example, choosing or making, we are then making use of our minds in a practical fashion.[51]

In the discussion to which we have referred, Thomas makes it clear that not just anything can be a concern of practical thinking, but only those things that we can do or make. That having been said, he suggests that while some instances of thinking may be called wholly theoretical and others wholly practical, it is often necessary to recognize that an instance of thinking can be in some respects theoretical and in other respects practical. Such mixed cases presuppose a plurality of criteria, and Thomas enumerates them in the following passage in which, though he is concerned with degrees of speculative thinking, he gives at the same time an account of degrees of practical thinking.

A given science can be called speculative in three ways: (1) First, *with respect to the things known*, which are not operable by the knower (that is, are not things he can do or make); this is the case with human knowledge of natural and divine things. (2) Second, *with respect to the mode of knowing*: as, for example, if a builder should consider a house by defining and distinguishing and considering its general description. This is to think of something makeable in a speculative or theoretical manner, not as makeable. A thing is makeable by the application of form to matter, not by an analysis of a complex thing into its universal formal principles. (3) Third, *with respect to the end*: for mind practical differs from mind theoretical in its end, as we read in the Third Book of *On the Soul*. The practical intellect is ordered to the end of operation whereas the end of the speculative intellect is the consideration of truth. Hence, if a builder should consider how a certain house might be built, not directing this to the end of operation, but to knowledge alone, his knowledge would thus be, with respect to his purpose, theoretical knowledge of an operable object.[52]

Taking this discussion in its applicability to human action as hitherto defined, such that it is clearly what Thomas means to include under his general term *operabile*, we can distinguish degrees of moral knowledge. A consideration of virtue, of justice, or of temperance that issues in definitions of these objects is practical only in the sense that it is concerned with things we might do, with achievable qualities of our actions. Nonetheless, because the mode of consideration is indistinguishable from that appropriate to a consideration of natural objects and provides no immediate guide to action, the purpose of the knower cannot be to apply such knowledge. Let us call this *minimally practical knowledge* or *theoretical moral knowledge*. Where both the object and the method of considering are practical, we may, making use of a label Thomas suggests elsewhere,[53] call it *virtual or habitual practical knowledge*. Where all three criteria of the practical are saved—an operable object, a compositive or recipe mode of considering it, and the actual application of the knowledge—we can speak of *completely practical knowledge*.

If we now ask ourselves what type of practical knowledge is exemplified by, say, the Second Part of the *Summa theologiae*, or how, given the above, Thomas might characterize the kind of knowledge expressed in Aristotle's *Nicomachean Ethics*, the answer, while complicated, is clear. We find in the moral part of the *Summa* instances of theoretical knowledge without qualification, insofar as man's nature and various aspects of human psychology as well as remarks about the divine nature may be come upon there. From the point of view of practical knowledge, we certainly find a good deal that is minimally practical, for example, such things as the definition of virtue and subdivisions of moral virtue and the "parts" of justice. All this, we may say, is necessary if there is to be any moral advice, where by moral advice we mean the kind of practical knowledge that is aimed at practice. In other words, moral philosophy or moral theology would seem to reach its *intrinsic* aim in the formulation of virtually practical knowledge. A moral discussion, even when it concludes with a prescriptive judgment as to what is to be done, does not itself provide an instance of the kind of doing it prescribes. That is, making a prescriptive

judgment as to how one might act temperately is not in itself a temperate act.

E. Natural Law

We can now locate the two remaining points of Thomas's moral doctrine that we wish to discuss. The Thomistic notion of natural law precepts bears on a type of virtually practical knowledge, whereas the notion of the practical syllogism arises from an analysis of purely practical knowledge. With respect to natural law, then, the point is that natural law precepts amount to judgments which express at the highest level of generality what we ought to do. Thomas maintains that there are certain judgments as to what we should do that everyone is capable of making.[54] What we shall do is, first, look at Thomas's theological or cosmic description of natural law, and, second, discuss the content of natural law as distinguishable from the wider setting in which it is first introduced.

The whole of creation is governed by God, a governance that is also called providence. Another way of speaking of it is as the eternal law which incorporates the divine plan for creatures.[55] If law thus measures the activities of creatures, who are measured by it, being measured by it is not itself an instance of law as Thomas uses the term here. This is puzzling for the modern mind, perhaps, in that when we hear the phrase "natural law" we are likely to think of regularities within the natural world. For Thomas, law is a promulgated rational ordination to the common good by one who has charge of the community.[56] Now, just as natural events may be said to be rational, not because of any reasoning on the part of physical objects, but because of the wise ordering of their creator, so the activities of natural entities are lawful, not because they rationally direct themselves, but because they are directed. Thomas uses the phrase "natural law" of those creatures which are not only rationally directed but which rationally direct themselves to an end. Such creatures are men. Natural law is thus describable as that participation in eternal law which is peculiar to rational creatures. Men are not merely directed by divine reason, as if their activities can be called rational only by extrinsic denomination; they direct themselves rationally and this self-direction involves another law, distinct from eternal law. This new law is natural law.

The view of man involved is one with which we are now familiar. The notion of human action is of deliberate volition, of conscious self-direction. Furthermore, as the discussion of human freedom made clear, man has not been given a mind simply to discover the single possible course of action open to him. Any choice bears on a course of action in which reason can discover pros and cons. Thus, we are not forced to act in the way we do. Nor is this merely an ontological openness, as if it meant simply that we are as capable of acting wrongly as of acting rightly. The indeterminancy involved is moral; there is no single map of good human action. Good courses of action must be discovered by reason. And yet we recall from the treatment of freedom derived from the concept of ultimate end that our freedom does not extend to the ultimate end itself. Thomas holds that a man necessarily desires his own happiness. It follows that true articulations of human happiness or perfection, true judgments as to the nature and constituents of the ultimate end, will give us the principles and starting points of moral discourse. It is these principles that are covered by the phrase "natural law" in its moral employment.

What is the import of the adjective "natural" when we speak of natural law?[57] As we shall see, it has at least a double valence. On the one hand, it suggests a law appropriate to our human nature, prescriptive judgments as to what is good for, what is perfective of, such an entity as ourselves. On the other hand, it has an epistemological meaning in that the judgments in question are ones that a man makes naturally, easily, right off the bat. Both of these senses are operative in a famous passage in which Thomas asks whether there is one only or several precepts of natural law.

It should be mentioned that there is only one place in the writings of St. Thomas where we find anything like an extended formal treatment of natural law. This occurs in the context of the so-called Treatise on Law in the *Summa theologiae*, the First Part of the Second Part, Questions 90–105. Thomas first takes up the question of the nature of law in general and arrives at the definition we have already given: law is a promulgated rational ordinance to the common good on the part of one having charge of the community. He then distinguishes types of law: eternal law, natural law, human law, and divine law. As the definition suggests, laws other than human positive law are said to be such by an analogy with it. The discussion of natural law is to be found in Question 94, although the discussions of human law and of divine positive law, particularly the discussion of the Ten Commandments, cast helpful light upon it.

When Thomas raises the question of the content of natural law—is it made up of one or of several precepts?—he employs an interesting parallel between the priorities and procedures of theoretical intellect and those of practical intellect.[58] The precepts of natural law, he holds, function for practical intellect in much the same way that self-evident truths function for the speculative or theoretical use of the intellect. Indeed, the precepts of natural law are themselves taken to be self-evident or *per se nota*; that is, they are known "in themselves" as opposed to being derived or inferred.

This notion of the "knowable in itself" is ambiguous, however, and can mean one of two things: knowable in itself as such, or knowable in itself by us. The first is had whenever a proposition is such that its predicate enters into the definition of its subject. Of course, when one does not know the definition of the subject, he will not recognize that the proposition is self-evident. The proposition "Man is rational" is self-evident, but if someone did not know that man is defined as a rational animal, he would not grasp the proposition as self-evident. Where knowledge of the definition of the subject term cannot be lacking, we have the sort of self-evident propositions that Boethius called axioms; these are such that no one could fail to know the meaning of their terms—for example, "Every whole is greater than its part" and "Two things equal to a third thing are equal to each other." The first sort of self-evident proposition, the non-axioms, are self-evident not to everyone but only to the knowledgeable. "An angel is nowhere" is such a proposition. Those who know that angels are not bodies immediately grasp the truth of the judgment that they are not circumscriptively in place, that is, that they do not take up any room.

It may be wondered what the significance of introducing this distinction is. Thomas has told us that he considers the precepts of natural law to be self-evident propositions. Are they self-evident in both of the ways explicated? That is, are there some principles of natural law that every man knows and others that are perceived as self-evident only by the learned? If this is the suggestion—and it is difficult from the context to be absolutely sure—then we must keep open the possibility that extremely sophisticated propositions, for example, those that prohibit the use of artificial contraceptives on the basis of the biology of reproduction and the chemistry of certain pills, may be matters of natural law and self-evident to the learned. However that may be, it is certain that in the immediate sequel to the distinction between kinds of self-evident propositions, the emphasis seems to be on those that are analogous to axioms in the theoretical order.

In the order of theoretical thinking, Thomas goes on, being is the first thing grasped by the mind, since knowledge of it is presupposed by and included in all subsequent knowledge. On the basis of this grasp of being, the first judgment is made: the same thing cannot be affirmed and denied; the same thing cannot be and not be at the same time and in the same respect. This, the so-called principle of contradiction, is the regulative principle of all our thinking, of all subsequent judgments and principles. The parallel to it in the practical order is this: good is the primary concept in the practical use of our mind. Every agent acts for an end, Thomas writes, and the end instantiates the notion of the good. The good is that which all things seek. On this initial grasp is based the first preceptive judgment of practical reason: the good is to be done and pursued, and evil is to be avoided. This principle is fundamental and regulative of all other precepts of natural law. What is the criterion for inclusion in the precepts of natural law? "All things which should be done or which should be shunned pertain to precepts of natural law insofar as practical reason naturally apprehends them to be human goods."[59]

The application of this criterion is of great interest. Practical reason will naturally apprehend as good, and thus as to be pursued while its opposite is to be shunned, all those things to which man has a natural inclination. Furthermore, the order of the precepts will follow that of natural inclinations: the hierarchy of the latter will be reflected in the former. What is meant by an order among our natural inclinations? This: there are certain inclinations, natural impulses, that we share with all things, for example, the impulse to preserve ourselves in being. There are other inclinations that we share with other animals, for example, the urge to mate and to raise offspring. Finally, there is in us an inclination to the good according to the nature of reason, and this is the inclination peculiar to us; for example, we have a natural inclination to seek the truth and to live in society.[60]

This is the ordered set of natural inclinations that Thomas says we find within ourselves. These inclinations are not themselves precepts of natural law; their importance is that their presence within us assures that we have immediate access to certain types of good, of objects of desire and inclination. But, again, the natural inclinations are not themselves precepts; if they were, the effort to distinguish natural from eternal law would have been unnecessary. It is when we turn to the third and last type of natural inclination, that which is proper to man, namely, to live according to reason, that we find the locus for natural law. The human agent, aware in his own experience of his desire for pleasure, feeling the urgency of the sexual instinct, must consciously guide himself with respect to such activity. He is not simply propelled into conjugation like a beast; he acts consciously, responsibly, with awareness in such matters; he foresees consequences, he must provide, and so on. Certain judgments as to how we must comport ourselves with respect to reproducing and raising children will immediately be made. It has been suggested that a first precept in this area need only be the recognition that some regulation of sexual intercourse is necessary if such activity is to be human, that is, rational.[61] Such further recognitions as that we must seek knowledge of the context of our deeds and that the rights of others are to be respected would be suggestive of the first and immediate judgments which guide human actions.

Needless to say, this doctrine of natural law is a vexed and controversial subject. Simple historical accuracy demands that

we attribute to Thomas only what he had to say on the matter
and not burden him with any and every later variation on it.
His own teaching on natural law seems to be at once clear
and obscure. It sounds right to say that there are objective
limits within which men can justifiably work out their lives,
that beyond these limits we would be unwilling to recognize
action as appropriately human. But the articulation of the first
self-evident precepts is difficult. Perhaps this is merely another
aspect of their similarity to the first principle of theoretical
reason. After all, however well it captures the regulative principle of all our thinking, the first time we encounter the
formulation, "It is impossible for a thing to be and not to be
at the same time and in the same respect," it strikes us as a
sort of tongue twister, nothing we would say untutored. And
yet it does, we come to see, express what no one could meaning-
fully deny. Given this, it may not harm the theory of natural
law precepts to say that whenever we attempt to articulate one,
we nevertheless have the sense of constructing an extremely
artificial formulation.

F.   Moral Science

A further implication of the parallel between the theoretical
and the practical would seem to be this: just as the principle
of contradiction is not a proper principle of any particular
science, since it ranges over all, so too the precepts of natural
law are the presuppositions of moral science. Indeed, this
appears to be a necessary interpretation, since Thomas on more
than one occasion speaks of moral science as capable of establishing only what is usually the case, for the most part true.
The conclusions of moral science, in other words, are general;
they express what is by and large the preferable way to act.
This matter of the relation between natural law precepts and
other moral precepts is one that Thomas discusses on several
occasions. The following passage is of considerable interest.

It should be known that something is derived from natural law in
two ways; first, as a conclusion from principles and, second, as the
determination of the common. The first mode is similar to the way

in which in sciences demonstrative conclusions are derived from principles. The second is similar to the way in which in the arts common forms are determined to something special, as the artisan determines the common form of house to this or that house. Some things are derived from the common principles of natural law by way of conclusion like this: "Thou shalt not kill" can be derived as a conclusion from "Do harm to no one." Some things are gotten by way of determination as follows: as the natural law has it that he who sins is punished, that he should be punished in such and such a way is a determination of the natural law.[62]

Although the first mode would seem to be itself a particularization, it is clear that Thomas envisages some such inference as:

(1) Do harm to no one.
(2) To kill someone is to do him harm.
(3) Do not kill anyone.

Not a very controversial example, perhaps, but this mode of derivation, as well as the other, suggests that Thomas thinks of moral science or knowledge as a progressive development, which has at one term, as its governing principles, the self-evident precepts of natural law, and moves toward more and more particular precepts. The development in the direction of particularity would seek the advantage of more concrete and applicable precepts.

This advantage is equivocal, however. The characteristic of the common self-evident precepts of the moral order is that they are the same for everyone, that they hold always and everywhere. Their disadvantage would seem to be one of interpretation. If it is taken to be obvious that one should harm no man, it is not always clear what harm is. The same, of course, is true of killing. Presumably, the kind of killing that is prohibited is what we should call murder. Now, to say that murder is always wrong, that one should never murder, is to say something that no doubt is always true, always applies. But this does not foreclose difficulties, because the determination of when killing is unjustified, of when it is murder, that is, is not always easy. Thus the need for a movement toward ever more circumstanced and particular precepts to overcome that difficulty of interpretation. But this in turn has its dark and disadvantageous side.

But with respect to the proper conclusions of practical reason, there is not the same truth and rectitude for everyone, nor are they even equally known by all. For everyone it is right and true that one must act rationally. From this principle follows as a proper conclusion, so to speak, that the goods of another should be returned. That is for the most part true, but in the particular case it can happen that it would be perilous, and thus irrational, to return another's goods; for example, if he asks for them in order to subvert the country. This defect increases as we get increasingly particular; for example, if we should say that goods should be returned but with these exceptions and in this manner. The more conditions we add, the more ways the precept can fail to apply, such that it will not be right either to return or not to return goods.[63]

So much for the ambiguous nature of moral science according to Thomas. The intrinsic goal of moral science is the most circumstanced knowledge possible of what we should do; the closer it comes to its objective, the more need for interpretation in the application of its precepts. And, of course, it is application, action, practice that is the ultimate goal of moral science, of the practical use of our mind.

G.   The Practical Syllogism

If moral science is virtually practical knowledge, this is because its considerations, no matter how nuanced and circircumstanced, remain on the level of generality. We have seen how Thomas holds that the more concrete, and thus helpful, the considerations of moral science become, the more difficult they are to apply, since so many qualifications have been built into the precept. This means that such a precept, insofar as it expresses ways and means of achieving our end or moral ideal, is problematic in the extreme. The view of the nature of moral science which thus emerges is striking. On the one hand, there are principles which express what is our perfection or end or ways of acting without which the end could not be achieved. The certitude of such judgments is bought at the price of great vagueness, however. To know that murder is always and everywhere wrong is to have an important truth, but it is of little value if we are not able to handle the extremely complicated situations in which men may find themselves and in which it is the identification of an action as murder that is the chief problem. Insofar as our inquiry attempts to overcome vagueness, it does so at the expense of certitude. Thus, at either end, moral knowledge seems to leave a lot to be desired and we are not surprised, perhaps, to find Thomas saying that moral science is of little or no value.[64]

What is the import of that remark? We must recall the nature of practical knowledge, of which moral science is an instance. The aim or end of practical knowledge is not to get our minds straight about the way things are. Rather, it is thought undertaken to guide actions so that *we* may become as we ought to be. The aim of theoretical knowledge is truth, Thomas says, and insofar as we say the same of practical knowledge, we shall want to alter the meaning of the term.

Truth in practical intellect is different from truth in the speculative intellect, as is pointed out in the Sixth Book of the *Ethics* (1139a26). The truth of speculative intellect consists in the mind's conformity with reality. Because the mind cannot be infallibly conformed to things in contingent matters, but only in necessary matters, no speculative habit of contingent matters is an intellectual virtue; these are confined to necessary matters. The truth of practical intellect consists in conformity with right appetite, a conformity which is irrelevant with respect to necessary things which are not due to human will, but only with respect to contingent matters which can be effected by us, whether it is question of interior actions or external artifacts. Thus the virtues of practical intellect bear on contingents, art on things to be made, prudence on things to be done.[65]

The prudence or practical wisdom which is here spoken of as a virtue of the practical intellect is not to be confused with moral science. The latter is concerned with contingent matters, but at a level of generality. Prudence bears on the singular circumstances in which one acts and thus may be thought of as the application of general truths to particular, singular circumstances. Like Aristotle before him, Thomas speaks of a practical syllogism, the discourse whereby one applies generalities to particular circumstances with a view to acting. The

major premise of the practical syllogism is a general precept
or law.[66]

Two kinds of knowing are directive of human acts, a universal and
a particular kind, for when we put our minds to thinking about
things to be done, we make use of a sort of syllogism, the conclusion of which is a judgment or choice or operation. Actions, after
all, are singular. Thus, the conclusion of an operative syllogism must
be singular. Now a singular proposition is derived from a universal
only by way of another singular proposition, as a man is prohibited
the act of parricide because he knows a father ought not be killed
and knows that this man is his father.[67]

Not only must we know general precepts, we must also know
their application to particular circumstances. The problem would
seem to be merely a cognitive one, but it can often be the case
that the reason such knowing does not take place is the condition
of the agent's appetite. One may assent to the general precept
as expressive of the way one should act given man's end, and
yet one's past history of action may incline one to act contrary
to the general precept. If a man is in a state of passion, drawn
by the promise of sense pleasure, say, he may well be dis-
inclined to see his circumstances in the light of the precept
which prohibits fornication. This failure to think is a species
of ignorance, and Thomas will thus see sin as a species of ignorance. But the ignorance need not be, as in our example it
is not, a failure to know the general precept. The failure of
knowledge in the case imagined has to do with these circumstances here and now. And the cause of the failure to apply
the general knowledge is an appetitive disposition, for example,
an acquired tendency or disposition to indulge oneself in matters
of sensual pleasure heedlessly. It is the reverse of this situation,
the happier possibility, that Thomas is envisaging when he
speaks, as in the passage quoted earlier, of practical truth. One
whose appetite is disposed to be directed by reason in matters
of sense pleasure is said to possess the virtue of temperance.
Thus the right appetite, conformity with which is practical truth,
turns out to be moral virtue. Moral virtue both removes impediments to and positively disposes one to the guidance of the

general moral precepts, knowledge of which may be due to moral science. Practical reason as guided by practical wisdom or prudence is thus seen to be dependent not only on cognitive prowess but also on an appetitive disposition.

When the practical syllogism is looked upon simply as a cognitive sequence, problems arise as to why choice or action is said to be the "conclusion" of such discourse. That fornication should not be committed and that this person is not one's spouse may be grounds for the recognition that one should not have sexual intercourse with the presumably pliable young lady in question. But why, it is often asked, should this inference be taken to issue in action? Is it not at best a cognitive recognition perfectly compatible with action contrary to it? Put thus, it is quite clear that the difficulty is unavoidable. If Thomas proceeds otherwise, it is because, for him, the practical syllogism is not simply a matter of knowledge.[68]

The so-called major premise of the practical syllogism is expressive of the human good, of that which is perfective of the kind of agent man is, either as his end or as means to the achievement of that end. *Knowledge* of the good is expressive of truth in the usual sense. But to relate to the *good as true*, to have merely a cognitive relation to it, is not to relate to it *as good*. The good is the object of appetite. It is only when the major premise of the practical syllogism expresses truly a good to which we also relate appetitively as good that the practical discourse will issue in action or choice as its conclusion.[69] In short, appetite, disposition, has to be present from the beginning if this is indeed to be an instance of practical discourse, of discourse aimed at practice, at action. If the major premise expresses a good to which we relate as a good, then the application expressed in the minor premise is facilitated and the conclusion which is an action follows. Only when the premises are taken to have to produce appetite, as it were, for the first time when the conclusion is reached do the unfortunately familiar difficulties arise.

This sketch of the moral doctrine of Thomas Aquinas will have to suffice for present purposes. It is of course tempting to add to the sketch from the vast number of pages Thomas devoted

to the presuppositions, concomitants, corrolaries, and consequences of the few matters we have mentioned. The hope is
that, however skeletal the presentation, it may nonetheless
serve to suggest the basic structure of Thomas's moral philosophy. One who knows Aristotle well will find much that is
familiar in the account we have given, and this is no accident.
And yet, as our discussion of ultimate end makes clear, Thomas
put the Aristotelian approach to the service of elucidating moral
theology as well as moral philosophy. When man's end is
recognized to be a supernatural one, the means to achieving it
can scarcely be thought of as virtues a man can acquire through
his natural capacities alone. Thus Thomas will speak of infused
as well as of acquired virtues.[70] Indeed, his moral theology, as
is only to be expected, gathers round the preeminent Christian
virtue of Charity. Man's ultimate purpose is to love God with
his whole heart and soul and his neighbor as himself. Reflection
on what this ennobling task consists of, reflection at the level
of generality as to how this aim can be realized, could never
be confused, as will be obvious, with the acts of charity that
are the ultimate concern of such reflection.[71]

CHAPTER 3

Thomas Aquinas and Boethius

UNTIL the introduction into the West of the complete works of Aristotle, something we have spoken of in previous chapters, one of the major conduits whereby Aristotle became known was Boethius. Anicius Manlius Severinus Boethius (480–524) has been called the last of the Romans and the first of the Scholastics. The description is apt because Boethius bridges, both in fact and by intention, the world of classical Greek philosophy become a Roman patrimony—though even in his day it had sunk to a pitiable condition—and the yet to be constructed medieval world, the world of the universities, traces of which are still present in our own day. Member of a notable Roman family, Boethius had both a public and a private career in that he was both politician and scholar. Under the Ostrogoth King Theodoric, Boethius held the office of consul as well as other traditional political offices. It was as the result of an accusation of treason, the charge that he had conspired with the emperor in Constantinople against the barbarian king, that Boethius was put to death in Pavia. *The Consolation of Philosophy*, the work that was to have such an immense influence on the Middle Ages, was written in his death cell. Thus, in a sense, Boethius's two careers finally blended and ended together.

Boethius, pained by the demise of philosophical culture, which at least in part was due to a declining knowledge of Greek, set himself the task of translating into Latin the complete works of Plato and Aristotle and then commenting on them in such a way that the thought of these two giants of antiquity would be seen to be complementary rather than opposed.[1] So far as we know, Boethius translated nothing of Plato, and of Aristotle he translated only the *Categories, On Interpretation,* and several other logical works. He also translated and wrote two commentaries

75

on Porphyry's *Isagoge*, an introduction to the *Categories* of
Aristotle, thus bequeathing to the Middle Ages the problem of
universals. Besides the *Consolation of Philosophy* and these translations and commentaries, Boethius also wrote five short theological works, on two of which Thomas Aquinas wrote commentaries. Just as it was possible to consider some major Thomistic
doctrines as arising out of the influence of Aristotle, so it is
possible to consider others as having a Boethian background or
setting.

The task that Boethius set himself—to show the essential unity
of thought between Plato and Aristotle—is reminiscent of Neoplatonism and, indeed, it has been shown that there is great
similarity, not to put too fine a point upon it, between the
writings of Boethius, the commentaries as well as the *Consolation*,
and the writings of such Neoplatonists as Porphyry and Ammonius.[2] Ammonius was teaching at Alexandria during the lifetime of Boethius, having come there from Athens, where he had
studied under Proclus. Pierre Courcelle has proposed the thesis
that Boethius was educated at Alexandria in the school of Ammonius, a fascinating hypothesis for the truth of which there is
strong evidence of a literary kind. The significance of this fact,
if it is a fact, is that it goes a long way toward explaining the
peculiar character of Boethius's interpretation of Aristotle. His
approach can be characterized as Neoplatonic and the penchant
of the commentaries can be tested by reference to the ostensibly
more independent works, the *Consolation* and the theological
tractates.

In this chapter, we shall be looking at Thomas's commentaries
on two Boethian theological tractates, the *De trinitate* (*On the
Trinity*) and another the medievals called the *De hebdomadibus*
but whose title is rather the question, *Whether Everything That
Is Is Good Just Insofar As It Is?* These commentaries were written, as we have seen, early in Thomas's career, and we can expect
to find in them a reading of Aristotelian doctrine as transmitted
by Boethius that will be controlled by Thomas's knowledge of
the Aristotelian corpus. This wider and independent knowledge
of Aristotle makes the commentaries of Thomas on Boethius
qualitatively different from the many that had been written
earlier, in the 11th and 12th centuries.[3] Of course our discussion

will not be confined to what Thomas had to say about the text of Boethius. That will merely be our springboard. Of principal interest will be the way in which the notion of *separatio* is introduced into the discussion of the relation of metaphysics to the other speculative sciences; the distinction between essence and existence, with its apparent dependence on the Boethian axiom, *Diversum est esse et id quod est* (what a thing is and that it is are diverse); and the compatibility of divine foreknowledge and human freedom. We are interested in Thomas's relation to Boethius as to a source of knowledge of Greek philosophy, a source he could assess by reference to his own independent knowledge of the writings of Aristotle. More important, however, we are concerned with the three major themes mentioned above which—although they have their counterparts in Boethius —in the hands of Aquinas achieve the kind of precise and clear treatment we have come to expect from him.

I *The Kinds of Speculative Science*

The commentary that Thomas began to write on the *De trinitate* of Boethius covers only its first chapter and part of the second. In this tractate, Boethius hopes to show, in terms of philosophical doctrine, how talk about God and the Trinity of Persons in God should be understood. Before getting to this task, however, he does a number of things, among them suggesting that in pursuing any inquiry it is well to know under what discipline it falls. Thus, at the outset of the second chapter, Boethius points out that theoretical or speculative considerations are of three kinds.

There are three kinds of speculative consideration, one of which, *natural philosophy*, deals with things in motion which cannot be abstracted from it (for it considers the forms of bodies along with their matter, which forms cannot actually be in separation from their bodies which are in motion, as earth is borne downward and fire upward). *Mathematics* is concerned with things without motion but which cannot be apart (for it speculates about forms of bodies without considering matter and consequently without motion, which forms since they are in matter cannot be separate from matter and motion). *Theology* is concerned with things without motion and which are separable and abstract (for the substance of God lacks both matter and motion).[4]

This is a dense passage that can only be understood against the background of the division into speculative and practical knowledge that we discussed in the preceding chapter. Given that division, we are here provided with Boethius's restatement of Aristotle's further subdivision of speculative knowledge into natural science, mathematics, and what has come to be called metaphysics. Before turning to that particular question and to the presentation of it that Thomas gives, we must first say a word about an ambiguity in Boethius's own position, a word that will indicate the importance of his own Neoplatonic predilections.

A. Boethius and Platonism

It has often been noted that elsewhere, namely in his first commentary on Porphyry's *Isagoge*, Boethius presents the three-fold division of speculative philosophy in a quite different manner than he does here.[5] The objects of the theoretical, he writes there, are three: intellectibles, intelligibles, and naturals. Intellectibles are described after the fashion of Platonic Ideas, while naturals are physical bodies and the changes they undergo. The difficulty resides in the middle class, the intelligibles. They do not seem to be, as in the *De trinitate*, mathematicals, for included in their number is the human soul. Boethius says of the intelligibles that, generally speaking, they were first intellectibles but because of contact with body they degenerated from the status of intellectible to the status of intelligible. The suggestion of a kind of falling away, of a cascade, from the most perfect being, through graded steps to matter, is Neoplatonic. But we do not have to look beyond the *De trinitate* itself for this kind of suggestion. In the second chapter of that work we read that forms that exist separately from body are true forms, while those that are in bodies come from those pure forms and ought rather to be called images than forms. Whatever the final significance of such remarks for Boethius's own thought—and it is obviously not our task here to determine that significance—enough has been said to indicate that Boethius is not a pure

Aristotelian and that, consequently, attempts to read his works from the viewpoint of strict Aristotelianism run the risk of going astray. Such is the accusation that has often been levelled at Thomas Aquinas, though it has more pertinence possibly to his commentary on the *De hebdomadibus* than to the commentary he wrote on the *De trinitate* of Boethius. The difference lies, at least in part, in the fact that these commentaries are of quite different types.

The commentary Thomas wrote on the *De hebdomadibus* is, like those he wrote on Aristotle and on Scripture, what could be called an extended exposition of the text. In commenting on the *De trinitate,* however, Thomas employs a literary form like that he used in commenting on the *Sentences* of Peter Lombard. That is, after an initial and brief indication of how the text is divided, he goes on to enumerate the questions it raises and then treats these questions more or less independently of the text which occasioned them. Thus, the whole of Question 5 in the commentary of St. Thomas deals with the dense passage we quoted above. For Thomas, this passage contains four major points for discussion. It is to what Thomas has to say on these points that we now turn, putting aside the question of Thomas's fidelity or lack of it to the thought of Boethius.

B. The Object of Speculation

In the preceding chapter, we saw the care with which Thomas set down the criteria for distinguishing speculative and practical thought. We are entitled to expect that he will show the same care in discussing how there can be different theoretical or speculative sciences. Our expectation will not be frustrated.

Let us, Thomas suggests, use the term *speculabile* to designate the object of the speculative concern of the mind. The concern of our mind in its practical mode is something we can do or effect in some way. As we saw in the preceding chapter, in pure speculative knowledge we are concerned with something which is not such an object, that is, which cannot be effected by us. Thus, we must say that our intellectual concern with what Thomas now calls the speculable object is not, since it cannot be, how to construct it, how to do it, but rather to see how and what it is: to arrive at the truth concerning it.

1. Intuition

This sort of language, the language of seeing, looking, contemplating, seems to suggest that for Thomas, theoretical thinking is a kind of intuition, a taking-a-look. While it is the case that our knowledge may be thought of as involving, by way of principle, starting point, or presupposition, such mere looking, Thomas was far more impressed by the need the mind has for an active process if it is going to discover how it is with things, their truth. When he speaks of speculative or theoretical knowledge, the emphasis seems to be far more on the discursive than on the intuitive. And it is just this notion of discourse that we need to have in mind if we are to follow Thomas through his exposition of Boethius here. It becomes very clear very soon that the vehicle of speculative knowledge for Thomas is what Aristotle called the apodictic, and what Thomas calls the demonstrative, syllogism Theoretical knowing is science, *scientia*, when it is achieved by means of such a discursive process.

What we have been calling intuition, Thomas would call *intellectus*,[6] a term he uses to speak of our grasp of a truth that is, so to say, self-warranting. Truth in its most common sense involves judgment; that is, when we think that something is the case and it is indeed the case, then our thinking or judgment is true. The verbal expression of such a judgment may be symbolized as S is P. Now, and again this is something we touched on earlier in speaking of the precepts of natural law, a judgment is what we have here called self-warranting (and Thomas would call *per se notum*) when to know what S is and to know what P is is to know the truth of the claim that S is P. Thomas would say that such a truth is *immediately* known. The adverb is being used logically and not temporally; that is, Thomas is not claiming, though neither is he denying, that such a judgment is known in a flash, swiftly, in the blink of an eye. When he says that it is known immediately, he has in mind its difference from the way in which the conclusion of a syllogism is known.

2. Scientific Knowing

Imagine that knowing what S is and knowing what P is do not suffice for knowing the truth of S is P. This instance of S is P is not immediately known, is not an object of *intellectus*. It may nonetheless be true and it may be known to be true. Its truth could be known in a variety of ways, but the way that interests us here is that which undergirds Thomas's use of "know" in the sense of *scire*, that which is productive of *scientia*, science, true and certain knowledge.

Before we can speak of the demonstrative or scientific syllogism, we must say something of syllogism itself. The Greek term from which the Latin and our English come first meant mental discourse, a knowing process, a coming to know. Aristotle's *Analytics* gave it a far narrower sense, at first technical but soon the ordinary or common or usual sense of the term. If the object of *intellectus* is expressed in one sentence, S is P, the syllogism is expressed in a suite or series of them: If C is said of every B, and B is said of every A, then C is said of every A. The very statement of the principle of syllogism conveys what we mean by discourse, process, coming to know. If we drop the hypothetical mode of expression and put the relations involved categorically, we would have:

(1) Every B is C
(2) Every A is B
(3) Every A is C

The third line, (3), stands for the conclusion that follows from or is derivable from the premises, (1) and (2). If the premises are true, the conclusion is true and its truth is dependent upon or derivable from theirs. It is clear that B is the hook, or link, between C and A, it is the means whereby (3) is seen to obtain. So we should say that (3) is known mediately. The connection between its predicate and subject is not known so soon as we know what each is; (3) is not known immediately. Mediate knowledge is thus intimately linked to syllogism where the middle term B is the medium whereby the major term C and the minor term A are linked in the conclusion.

We cannot here dwell on the nature of the syllogism, but it will be appreciated that since in the example we have been using all the sentences comprising it are universal affirmative ones, all we need do is imagine the variations that would follow on introducing particular and negative propositions to see how thin a presentation we have given. The example we have provided is a syllogism in the First Figure; that is, the middle term is the subject of the major premise and the predicate of the minor premise. One can see that other arrangements of the middle term are possible, for example, as subject term in both premises.

But inadequate as our remarks on the syllogism are, they may yet suffice for our purposes. Our purpose is to grasp what Thomas is saying in his exposition of Chapter Two of Boethius's *De trinitate*, where the Roman author is recalling, as it seems, Aristotle's classification of speculative or theoretical knowledge into types. Thomas has begun by saying that the object of theoretical knowledge can be given the name or designation, *speculabile*. In order for there to be kinds or types of *speculabile* and thereby kinds or types of theoretical knowing or science, we need to know what belongs to the speculable as such and, having found this out, to ask what variations in its essential or characteristic notes are possible. Our excursus into the nature 'of the syllogism has been meant to prepare the setting for Thomas's discussion of this: the natural habitat of the speculable is the demonstrative syllogism.

First, then, what belongs to the speculable as such? The "as such" is crucial. If we were asked to mention types or shades of green, the answer "hats and grass and hospital gowns" would not be an as-such answer. Green is not classifiable into shades in terms of objects that happen to be green. So too, if we wish to ask whether there are distinct types of speculative or theoretical knowings, distinct theoretical sciences, the distinction should be made in terms of what pertains to the object of such knowing, to the *speculabile*, as such. And what is that? Thomas holds that there are two things which pertain to the object of speculative or theoretical knowing as such, one of them deriving from the faculty or capacity in play, namely, the intellect, the other deriving from that which qualifies or perfects the intellect in this activity, namely, science.[7]

Already, in our discussion of the immortality of the human soul, we have seen something of what Thomas means by saying that our minds know whatever they know in an immaterial fashion. It is because he holds this to be true that Thomas can say that it will be a characteristic of the object of theoretical thinking that it is immaterial. From the side of science, Thomas suggests, another characteristic pertains to the speculable as such, and that is necessity. This takes us back to the demonstrative or scientific syllogism.

A judgment that is not self-warranting can nonetheless be known to be true. If we assert that snow is white, we mean our assertion to be true, and our warrant for its truth would be that we have never seen nonwhite snow. Of course we have seen dirty snow and snow which when Christmas lights reflect on it, looks red and green and blue and other colors, but we would not take this to count against our claim. We might, on the other hand, assert that the blossoms of flowering dogwoods are white, meaning that all flowering dogwoods have white flowers, and this would be false, our experience having been limited apparently to only one kind of flowering dogwood. Judgments that happen to be true or happen to be false are not self-warranting, and the basis of our claim that they are true or false may simply be such experiential evidence as leads us to speak as we do. But in the case of parallel lines, in Euclidean geometry, we would not of course say that it is true that parallel lines never meet because we have never seen any that do. What we mean by parallel lines are lines that do not meet no matter how extended on a plane. Thus, this is a self-warranting claim, *per se notum*. If now one takes the claim that the interior angles of a plane triangle equal 180°, this is not a self-warranting claim, although it is necessarily true. Taken as a theorem, we can cite reasons why it cannot be the case that the interior angles of a plane triangle fail to equal 180°. That is the sort of necessity Thomas has in mind when he speaks of the second characteristic of the speculable object. When we know something in the strong sense (*scire, scientia*), what we know does not just happen to be the case; it cannot not be the case; it is a necessary truth. Not every syllogism leads to a conclusion of that sort; the kind that does is called an apodictic or demonstrative or scientific syllogism.[8]

3. Modes of Defining

What Thomas is taking Boethius to be saying is this: there are formally different speculative sciences. In other words, not

every necessary conclusion is of the same type. But, as the
example of green and its shades was meant to show, he expects
this claim to be a formal one, one that relies on what pertains
to the speculable as such. But what pertains to the speculable
as such, he observes, is that it is (a) immaterial and (b) necessary. He now adds that what is necessary is unchangeable. The
changeable is that which can be otherwise than it is; the
necessary is that which cannot be otherwise. Therefore, if we
are going to claim that there are formally different speculative
sciences, we are going to have to show that there are different
ways in which objects of speculation are separated from matter
and motion. Separation (*separatio*) from matter and motion
pertains to the speculable as such. So, insofar as there is an
order or gradation or difference in removal (*remotio*) from
matter and motion, there is a basis for speaking of formally
different objects of theoretical thinking and, derivatively, of
formally different theoretical sciences. It is against this back-
drop, carefully and formally constructed, that he now gives his
own statement of the content of the passage from Boethius.

(1) *Some speculables* are such that they depend on matter in order
to be, because they can only exist in matter, and these are subdivided,
because (a) some of these are such that they depend on matter
both to be and to be understood, for example, those in whose definitions sensible matter is included; thus they cannot be understood
without sensible matter. Flesh and bones, for example, must be put
into the definition of man. *Physics* or natural science is concerned
with speculables of this sort. (b) Others are such that while they
depend on matter in order to be, do not depend on it in order to be
understood since sensible matter is not put into their definitions,
things like lines and numbers. *Mathematics* is concerned with speculables of this sort. (2) *There are some speculables* which do not
depend on matter in order to be, since they can exist apart from it,
whether they are never in matter, like God and the angels, or sometimes are and sometimes are not in matter, like substance, quality,
being, potency, act, one and many, and the like, with all of which
theology is concerned, that is, divine science, God being its chief
concern; it is also called *metaphysics*, that is, beyond physics, because
we who learn about the insensible from the sensible must study it
after we have learned physics.[9]

We have here another example of the extremely formal way in which Thomas approaches a subject. His writings have a surface simplicity, a kind of limpidity that may seem like shallowness; yet that simplicity is a means of density and depth. It is not only that he must, in any given discussion, presuppose things, as here he presupposes the immateriality of intellection and the necessity of the object of science, though such presuppositions are inevitable, and, in expositions such as this, it is important to draw attention to them. It is also true that, when he is granted the presuppositions he requires, Thomas proceeds in a manner whose formality is breathtaking. By "formality" I mean, of course, the logical elegance of his manner. Thomas is not the kind of author who is intent on concealing the seams and connections in what he has to say. The linkages, the skeleton, is close to the skin of his style. This makes reading him at once easy and difficult. Easy, because he is usually painstakingly clear as to what he thinks follows from what, which facilitates the testing and assessing of what he says. But difficult too, because his style permits a great deal of condensation. There are not only no *longueurs,* there are almost no paragraphs meant to relieve the reader—the kind of paragraph I am writing now—to amuse or divert him. Thomas was, as has been mentioned, capable of introducing rhetoric and poetry into his style, but when his purpose is, as it almost always was, to convey what he knows and to get us to know it too, he makes few concessions to a limited attention span. Such writers invite commentary and exposition, the spelling out of what in them is terse and tight. Oddly enough, they are also subject to much misinterpretation.

What we have just seen Thomas do is provide us with as formal a statement as he could fashion of the way in which we can speak of formally distinct speculative sciences. The tradition in which he moves speaks of natural science, mathematics and a further science, call it theology or divine science or metaphysics. It would be possible simply to take these as more or less traditional divisions of intellectual labor. We are amused by the man who is surprised to learn that he has been speaking prose all his life without knowing it. But it is also possible to know that one is speaking prose without being able to assign formal criteria for prose whereby it is distinguished from verse.

So too one might be able to distinguish natural science and mathematics, in the sense that one would correctly identify this argument as belonging to natural science and that argument as belonging to mathematics, and still not be able to say just what it is that characterizes a natural argument or just what characterizes a mathematical one. Thomas demands of his own tradition that it deliver up criteria for the distinctions it makes. His confidence is rewarded, as in the present instance, for he takes what he has said to be what both Aristotle and Boethius meant.

The setting forth of the criteria for distinguishing speculative sciences and the summary statement of the three speculative sciences form the burden of the first article of Question 5 of Thomas's exposition of the *De trinitate* of Boethius. There are three further articles in this question in which Thomas treats special difficulties that arise in applying the proposed accounts to natural science, to mathematics, and, finally, to divine science. In Article 2, he asks whether natural philosophy is, as has been urged, concerned with things that require matter and motion both in order to exist and in order to be defined. In the third article, he asks if mathematics defines without matter things that require matter in order to exist. Finally, in Article 4, he asks if divine science treats things that are not only defined without matter and motion but that exist independently of matter and motion. He thus unpacks and expands the doctrine we have seen developed in a preliminary and schematic way. We shall not, of course, follow those further developments in detail. Rather, we shall concentrate on the claims and controversies concerning Thomas's notion of metaphysics as it emerges out of things said in the third article of Question 5.

4. Degrees of Abstraction?

We have seen how Thomas, having said that separation from matter and motion pertains to the speculable as such, concludes that, insofar as there are distinct modes of such separation, there are distinct speculative sciences. This has sometimes been referred to as a theory of degrees of abstraction from matter, a manner of speaking that is open to, and has received, much objection.[10] Thus, understood in a fairly wooden way, St.

Thomas might be taken to teach the following. Take a material object, say, an apple. First, abstract from its singular and individual traits the traits which make it to be *this* apple. You are left with the nature of apple, with that which makes an apple to be an apple, the kind or sort of thing it is. Second, abstract from, strip away, the characteristics of apple, but retain such notes as extension, sphericity, and the like, and you have the basis for geometry. Third, strip away such spatial extension and you have left only the subject of extension, the subject of physical and mathematical properties, namely, substance. Now, this would of course be a Lockean understanding of substance. Thomas himself, insofar as this travesty is meant to move us by degrees to theology or divine science, took it to mean that knowledge of God lurks in anything, since when we strip away the physical and the mathematical we are left with substance in the sense of divine substance. Thomas thought this misunderstanding to be stupid.

Now if this misunderstanding is to be avoided, we will need a correct understanding of what makes metaphysics or theology possible. Commentators on Thomas have insisted, particularly since the various drafts of this exposition of Boethius became known, on the terminology encountered in Article 3.[11] There Thomas speaks of metaphysics, not in terms of abstraction, but in terms of separation. This, we are told, is of the highest importance.

C. Abstraction, Separation, and Metaphysics

The importance must be carefully stated of course. We have already seen Thomas use the term *separatio* to cover any and all removal (*remotio*) or distancing from matter and motion, whether it is a question of natural science, mathematics, or metaphysics. These are introduced, in Article 1, as involving variations in the *separatio* required of any speculable. We can expect, then, that in Article 3 *separatio* must be being used in a special and narrower sense if it is to characterize the procedure of metaphysics as opposed to those of natural science and mathematics. And that is just what we do find. As a matter of fact, we find three terms in play, namely, distinction (*distinctio*), abstraction (*abstractio*), and separation (*separatio*), all having to do with the way in which the object of theoretical thinking relates negatively to matter and motion. We also find that two of these terms, namely, abstraction and separation, have both a common or broad sense and a narrow and more technical sense. It is in a narrow and technical sense, which he is at pains to provide, that Thomas now holds that *separatio* is peculiar to metaphysics. We must take equal pains to understand him aright.

1.   Two Mental Acts.

There are two different mental acts that must not be confused, Thomas begins: that whereby we know what a thing is, its nature, knowledge expressible in a definition, and that whereby, employing composition and division, we make affirmative or negative judgments. I may be said to abstract one thing from another, according to this second kind of mental activity, when I say "X is not Y." Here I am abstracting X from Y and, Thomas says, abstracting in this sense is permissible only if it is true that X is separate from Y. Better to call such abstraction separation, he suggests, since it implies separation in reality. The mental act whereby we consider what a thing is does not have the same implication, since I can, for example, consider the color red without considering the apple whose color it is, but I am not thereby committed to saying that red or redness exists apart from the apple, apart from things that are red. To think apart what does not exist apart is to consider it abstractly: this is abstraction in the narrow sense.

Very well. A terminological point. Our mind, Thomas says, distinguishes (*distinctio*) one thing from another in different ways. According to that mental activity which expresses itself in definition, the mind can distinguish A, can think A without thinking B, even though A exists together with B; to think apart what cannot exist apart is abstraction (*abstractio*) in the narrow sense. According to that mental activity which expresses itself in propositions, in judgments that are true or false, we can distinguish one thing from another, that is, say "A is not B," only if in fact A and B are separate; this kind of distinguishing is called separation (*separatio*) in the narrow sense.

All this is clear enough. Separation, in the narrow sense, is expressed in a negative judgment, the implication of which is that the subject exists separately from what occupies the predicate role in the sentence. This can be exemplified, as it is by Thomas, by "Man is not an ass." What all this has been introduced for, however, is to provide a new way of seeing the distinction of the speculative sciences. If we recall the way that Thomas laid out the three speculative sciences above, we will see that the mode of defining was the clue. Natural science considers things that cannot exist apart from matter and motion and that cannot be understood or defined without sensible matter. Mathematics considers things apart from sensible matter that exist in sensible matter. Now, if we stop here, we can easily put the earlier statement together with what Thomas says in Article 3 about abstraction. In the first place, given the notion of demonstrative syllogism, this emphasis on mode of defining seems right. The strongest instance of a demonstrative syllogism would be one whose conclusion attributes a property to a subject and whose middle term is the definition of the subject. A property being an accident which belongs to something just insofar as it is what it is, an accident will be seen to be a property only with reference to the definition of the subject.[12] Thus we might say that the subject of the conclusion of the demonstrative syllogism is the subject of the science, and that the conclusion is the object or aim of science.[13] The mode of defining, with reference to what is characteristic of the speculable, will give us different sciences, different subject matters, their difference residing precisely in the kinds of definition in play. Of course, a plurality of demonstrative syllogisms employing the same mode of defining will collectively make up one science.[14]

2. Two Kinds of Abstraction

If we return to the discussion of abstraction in the narrow sense, that is, to the consideration of A without considering B even though A does not and cannot exist apart from B, we find Thomas speaking of two kinds of abstraction, the abstraction of whole from parts, and the abstraction of form from matter. And there are, of course, restrictions on abstraction in this sense.

When then that through which the definition of a nature is constituted, that through which it is known, has an order to or dependence
upon something else, it is clear that the nature cannot be understood without that other:

    a) whether they be conjoined as the part is conjoined to the
        whole, as the foot cannot be understood apart from animal,
        because that whereby a foot is a foot depends on that where-
        by an animal is an animal;

    b) or conjoined as form is conjoined to matter, as part to part,
        or accident to subject, as the snub cannot be understood
        apart from nose;

    c) or even really separate things, as father cannot be under-
        stood without understanding child, though these relations
        exist in diverse things.[15]

When the understanding of a thing does not depend upon understanding something else, then the mind can abstract in the
present sense of that term.

    a) And not only when they exist separately, like man and
        stone, but even when they are really conjoined;

    b) whether as part and whole are conjoined, as the letter can
        be understood without syllable, but not vice versa, and the
        animal without foot, but not vice versa;

    c) or conjoined as form is conjoined to matter, and accident to
        subject, as whiteness can be understood without man, and
        vice versa.[16]

The twofold division of abstraction in the narrow sense, abstraction of whole and abstraction of form, Thomas goes on to
apply to natural science and mathematics, respectively. The
mathematician's consideration of quantified being is taken to
involve the abstraction of form because of the order in which
accidents inhere in substance.[17]

If it seems fairly unsurprising that Thomas should assign the
"abstraction of form" to mathematics as more or less peculiar
to it, the assignment of "abstraction of the whole" to natural
science is considerably less perspicuous.[18] What Thomas means
by abstracting a whole would seem to be involved in any and
every science. Indeed, the very examples he uses makes this
clear. Thus he wants to say that there are some parts which

enter into the understanding and definition of a whole and from which therefore we cannot abstract in knowing that whole, whereas we can of course abstract a whole from those of its parts on which an understanding of it is not dependent. We cannot understand what a syllable is without bringing in letters, or a compound without implying elements. On the other hand, we can understand a circle without reference to semicircles, though we cannot understand a triangle without reference to lines. Parts requisite for the understanding of a whole may be called *formal parts,* and those not requisite, *material parts.* Flesh and bones are formal parts of man; finger and toe, indeed *this* flesh and *these* bones, are not. The defined whole thus emerges as the universal, and the parts from which it is abstractable, its material parts, as the particular.

And thus there are two sorts of intellectual abstraction; *one* which answers to the union of form and matter, or of accident and subject, and this is the abstraction of form from sensible matter; *another* which answers to the union of whole and part, which is the abstraction of the whole whereby the nature is considered absolutely, according to its essential nature, and without the parts which are accidental to it because they are not parts of its species.[19]

It is because mathematics too presumably must abstract the universal whole from particulars, that is, consider circle apart from this circle or that, that the appropriation of this second kind of abstraction to natural science surprises. Thomas himself draws attention to the flaws in this appropriation. Nonetheless, a point has been reached in our discussion where controversy must be taken into account.

3. The Controversy

Thomas began by saying that we can think about one thing without thinking about another in two ways. In one way, by expressly setting aside the second, by saying that X is not Y. Here we are saying that X can be considered apart from Y because it exists independently or separately from Y. In another way, we think about X without thinking about Y, even though X does not exist apart from Y. This is what he means by abstraction in the narrow sense. The conjunction X/Y, which abstraction does not deny, may be a conjunction of form and matter (accident and subject) or of whole and part. The two kinds of abstraction based on these two kinds of conjunction can be exemplified both in natural and mathematical science; nonetheless Thomas appropriates the abstraction of form to mathematics and the abstraction of the universal whole to natural science. Now we can see what textual symmetry demands. We have run out of kinds of abstraction, but we still have one more speculative science. But there was a kind of mental distinguishing that was mentioned prior to the discussion of abstraction, namely, separation. Let us then appropriate separation to metaphysics. That is just what Thomas does.

As with the kinds of abstraction, separation can be exemplified in sciences other than that to which it is appropriated. Thus, in Thomas's early example, "Man is not an ass" is an example of *separatio,* as would be "A triangle is not discrete quantity." Since *separatio* is expressed in a negative judgment, we must ask just what negative judgment Thomas had in mind when he appropriated separation to metaphysics. It has sometimes been suggested that the separation he has in mind is that of essence from *esse* or existence. But this will not do, as we shall see. The context requires that the separation be from matter and motion, and this not only in understanding but in reality as well. That is to say, metaphysics reposes on the truth of the judgment that there exist things independent of, separate from, matter and motion.

Is there any need for a theoretical science beyond natural science and mathematics? That is the way the question is put by Aristotle. He rejected, as Thomas in turn will do,[20] the suggestion that our understanding of natures independently of notes of particularity argues for the existence of a realm of entities distinct from the particular things of our sense experience. That we might think of man, of human nature, without adverting to what is peculiar to this man or that, to Socrates as Socrates or to Plato as Plato, does not entail that there is an entity, Man, who exists independently of our consideration and separately from Plato and Socrates. This is one solution to the so-called Problem of Universals, which we will be considering in our next chapter. No more does mathematics argue for the existence of another realm of things apart from physical objects. Thus, one possibility of generating a third speculative science would be to say that it is a third way of considering physical objects.

Now while this seems to take us back to the conception of degrees of abstraction as a way of understanding the distinction of the theoretical sciences, it does seem to be necessary to say that metaphysics is yet another way of thinking about the objects diversely thought about by natural science and mathematics. The subject of metaphysics is said to be, in the Aristotelian phrase, being as being, *ens inquantum ens.* The degree or gradation view of the theoretical sciences would then characterize their subjects as: (a) being as sensible or being as mobile; (b) being as quantified; and (c) being as being. And this suggests that metaphysics is a kind of general science, a yet more universal way of considering what is considered by natural science and mathematics. And then, just as mathematics does not argue for the existence of a realm of nonphysical objects, metaphysics would not argue for the existence of objects other than the physical objects of our sense experience. Call this conception of metaphysics ontology. But clearly Thomas wants to allow for the existence of things that are not physical objects, things that exist separately from matter and motion, things like God and the angels. If metaphysics is concerned with such things, our conception of it will be as a theology, a divine science. Which of these conceptions of metaphysics does Thomas choose? As we shall see at length in Chapter 5, he chooses both, or, more accurately, he rejects the meaningfulness of the proposed option. If metaphysics is concerned with God, as it is, God is nonetheless not the subject, nor part of the subject, of the science; rather, God enters into the science as the cause of its subject. The subject of metaphysics, being as being, must therefore be yet another way of viewing physical objects.

A fuller explanation of the Thomistic position on this matter will be attempted later. We must now discuss a matter which has been referred to in our remarks on the exposition of the *De trinitate* of Boethius but which is a concern of another Boethian work, the *De hebdomadibus*: the distinction of essence and *esse.*

II *Essence and Existence*

While few would maintain that Thomas was the first to teach that in things other than God, in creatures, their nature or essence is distinct from their existence—that is, only God is such that, given *what* he is, it is thereby given *that* he is—it seems clear that no one prior to Thomas made such constant reference to this truth or employed it in so many ways as the source of other truths. When we turn to Thomas's predecessors, however, we find a good deal of controversy among scholars as to where precisely they made the distinction in question. With Boethius, it is comparatively easy to cite the place. It is in his *De hebdomadibus* that we find the phrase Thomas will so often quote: *diversum est esse et id quod est*: what a thing is and that it is are diverse. Boethius, it has been argued,[21] does not mean by this phrase what Thomas in his exposition takes him to mean. Our principal interest here of course is to discover what Thomas took Boethius to mean.

A. The Boethian Axiom

The treatise of Boethius sets out to answer the question, whether everything that is is good just insofar as it is. In other words, is for a thing to be the same as for a thing to be good? A difficult problem, and one that Boethius proposes to approach *more geometrico,* which is to say that he will first set down axioms necessary for the resolution of the question and then, taking the question as a theorem, resolve it. It is among these axioms that we find the phrase that interests us because it interested Thomas so much, namely, *diversum est esse et id quod est*: what a thing is and that it is are diverse. In what way are they diverse? Boethius, as Thomas reads him, gives three differences.[22] First, existence (*ipsum esse*) does not exist; rather, what-is (*quod est*), having received a form of being, is and subsists. Second, what-is can share in or partake of other things, whereas existence (*ipsum esse*) does not share or participate in anything else: existence is that which what-is participates in in order to be. Third, what-is can possess what is not part of or identical with itself, whereas existence cannot. Thomas insists that this threefold diversity of the subject of being and existence is conceptual, a matter of what we understand by the terms. Indeed, he will exemplify the two with a variety of abstract and concrete terms. Thus, what-is, for example, white, that which has whiteness, differs from whiteness. Likewise, the runner is diverse from running. There are conceptual differences between the members of such couplets, precisely the three differences mentioned in the preceding paragraph. Whiteness does not exist, but that which has whiteness does. That which has whiteness can share in temperature, weight, and so forth, but whiteness as such is not hot or cold, heavy or light. What has humanity (man) and humanity exhibit the same differences.

What precisely is being distinguished here? It is often said that all Boethius is distinguishing is nature and individual. That is, it is pretty clear that what-has-humanity, Socrates, for example, is not identical with humanity, with what-it-is-to-be-a-man. However important this distinction, call it the distinction between nature or essence and individual or supposit,[23] it does not seem to be what Thomas himself has in mind when he talks about the difference between, or the composition of, essence and *esse*. How does Thomas argue that that-which-has-existence and existence differ really and not merely conceptually?

When that-which-has-existence is in itself composite, as any natural thing is, since it is a compound of matter and form, then, Thomas argues, it is clear that that-which-has-existence is really different from existence. Here is his argument.[24]

(1)   Existence itself (*ipsum esse*) does not partake of or participate in anything.

(2)   Existence itself cannot have anything extraneous: it cannot be the subject of an accident.

(3)   Therefore existence itself is not composed, is not compound.

(4)   Therefore no composed thing is identical with its existence.

(1) and (2) are taken from the axioms Boethius set down and which have already been analyzed by Thomas. (3) is a direct consequence of them, on the assumption that the modes of complexity denied *ipsum esse* in (1) and (2) are exhaustive of relevant complexity and thus warrant the denial which (3) is.

It is the transition from (3) to (4) that may seem problematic.
Why does it follow from the fact that existence *itself* is not composed that no composed thing is identical with *its* existence?

(5)   That-which-has-existence, an existent thing, a being,
       is designated such from its existence.
(6)   A being is composed of that-which-has existence and
       the existence it has.
(7)   That which exists is not existence alone.
(8), Its existence is simple, noncompound.
(9)   That-which-has existence is not its existence, is dis-
       tinct from, diverse from, it.

In propositions (5)–(9), that which exists may be either in
itself composed, that is, a composite of matter and form, or it
might conceivably be form alone. In other words, we have here
a more generalized form of the argument (1)–(4). Whenever
existence is the existence of something, there is a distinction
between what is and existence—not merely a conceptual distinction, but a distinction *realiter*.[25] Thus a simple or noncomposed
essence, form alone, enters into an existent thing as one component of it distinct from existence as another component. As a
being, therefore, it is composed, even though its essence is not
a composed essence. A truly simple being would be one in
which there is no composition of essence and existence, a being
in which existence would not be the existence *of* something, inherent, but rather subsistent existence. There can be only one
simple being of this kind.

This however would be unique, because if *ipsum esse* has nothing
admixed with it and is nothing other than existence itself, it is impossible that it be diversified or multiplied. . . . This one and sub-
lime simple thing is God himself.[26]

Elsewhere, in another early work, *On Being and Essence*,
Thomas gives a much simpler and more straightforward version
of his doctrine of the real distinction between essence and
existence.

Whatever does not enter into the understanding of an essence or
quiddity comes to it from without and enters into composition with
the essence, since no essence could be understood without the parts

that make it up. Every essence or quiddity, however, can be understood without its being understood that it exists in fact: for I can understand what a man or a phoenix is and yet not know whether they are given in reality. Therefore, it is clear that existence is other than essence or quiddity, unless indeed there should be some thing whose quiddity is its existence; and such a thing could only be unique and first.[27]

It seems clear enough that natural things do not exist by definition, as if existence were what they are or part of what they are, since, if that were so, they could not not be. But natural things are simply things which come into being, then cease to be. If there is something which exists by definition, which cannot not exist, it is unique and first, it is God.

The matters we have just been considering are easily the most difficult and arcane of any that we have considered or will be considering in this book. But to ignore a doctrine so central to the thought of Thomas Aquinas, one which caused controversy in his own time and has continued to do so ever since, would have been irresponsible. Unfortunately, it is impossible to give an account of it that is both succinct and cogent. The upshot of the teaching is quite clear. God alone is a being for whom to be is *what* he is; God alone is such that he cannot not be. He is, in short, a necessary being.[28] Whatever other than God exists does so, not because it is of its nature to exist, a definitional necessity, as it were, but because it has received existence. This upshot of the real distinction between essence and existence is one to which we shall be returning.

B. Separation and the Real Distinction

We must now ask what is the connection, if any, between the real distinction of essence from existence and that *separatio* which Thomas took to be characteristic of metaphysics. We have already mentioned that some have said that Thomas means to say that metaphysics commences at the moment that we recognize the real separation of essence and existence.[29] In this view, the negative judgment expressive of *separatio* would be: essence is not existence. If it is asked how this enables us to see what the subject of metaphysics is, the answer has been that essence is

the subject of natural science, whereas *esse*, or existence, is the
subject of metaphysics. Now, quite apart from the fact that this
leaves mathematics unaccounted for, it will not do because it
simply does not mesh with the doctrine in Thomas's exposition of
the *De trinitate* of Boethius.

The subjects of the various speculative sciences are distinguished insofar as their definitions diversely remove them from
matter and motion. The definition of the subject of natural
philosophy abstracts from particular sensible matter, but common or universal sensible matter is part of the natures studied.
The definition of the subject of mathematics does not include
sensible matter, common or particular, but no assertion is
made that there exist, apart from our consideration and apart
from physical bodies, subsistent lines, circles, triangles, and
so forth. It is into this general development that the notion of
separatio has to be fitted. The subject of metaphysics is defined
in such a way that no matter enters into the definition, with
the implication that there are existent things which respond as
such to such definitions. That is, the negative judgment that
is expressive of the *separatio* in question is: not every existent
thing is material and mobile. For Thomas, metaphysics becomes
a possibility, there is seen to be need for a science beyond
natural science and mathematics, when and if we can demonstrate that not every existent thing is a physical thing. Examples
of such a demonstration would be (a) that the human soul,
which is immaterial, continues to exist after death, and (b)
that there is a first unmoved mover. He finds such demonstra-
tions in Aristotle and he takes it to be highly important that they
are found in works devoted to natural philosophy.[30] The proofs
which are the prerequisites of metaphysics are achievements
of an ongoing natural science.

Thus far in this chapter, we have taken the occasion of
Thomas's exposition of two tractates of Boethius to discuss two
fundamental Thomistic doctrines. The first concerned the
criteria for distinguishing the theoretical sciences. We are
committed to returning to the question of metaphysics in a
later chapter in order to resolve the question whether it is best
thought of as an ontology or as a theology. Second, prompted
by an interpretation given to the technical term *separatio* as it

occurs in the exposition of the *De trinitate*, we discussed the real distinction between essence and existence. We turn now to a third point, almost as difficult as these, alas, which is discussed by Boethius in *The Consolation of Philosophy*,[31] the problem of determinism. Thomas did not comment on this work, but he did comment on the work of Aristotle which is one of its sources.

III   *Omnipotence, Omniscience, and Free Will*

That men act freely and are thus answerable for what they do is one of those assumptions so basic that to formulate it is to adopt a platitudinous air. Praise, blame, reward, and punish-ment—the whole network of morality and society—would be nonsense if man were not free. The individual is often tempted to think the contrary, of course; there are times when it would be convenient to think that we could not not have acted as we did, that some force, power, or fate, of which we were the mere pawns, was working itself out through us. Of course, the sense of innocence that such a thought may mistakenly induce would be, granting the truth of the temptation, as absurd as the guilt it exorcises. There are other less self-serving ways in which our thoughts might turn upon this fundamental assumption of free-dom and wonder if it is so. Now the wonder would arise from the assumption's being so if something else is so. For example, someone might hold that all material things are governed by natural law; that every event has a cause and that, if only we knew enough, we would see that each and every natural event comes about necessarily. Human freedom becomes problematic when it is doubted that there is any aspect of human behavior that escapes the material, natural world. If human free acts are only natural events in the sense just described, it would seem that they come about necessarily. But does that make sense? Can an action be such that it is both free and yet could not not have been performed?

The believer has what can only be called a more acute ver-sion of this difficulty. The Christian vocation makes no sense unless men freely respond to it, and that means that they could equally well have not responded to it. To accept God's word

and to act in accord with it is praised and rewarded; to defy
God's will is blamed and punished. Can one be praised or
blamed for what one could not not have done? Surely not. Thus,
Christianity sees man as a center of freedom, responsible for
the condition that will be his eternally. And, of course, the
Christian believes in God's providence; he believes that God
knows all things and can do all things. From these great truths
of the faith, arises the problem: Are they compatible with each
other? Is the set of them consistent? If God knows from all
eternity that I will choose this rather than that, is my choice
free?

A. The Divine Omnipotence

What does it mean to say that God can do all things, that
all things are possible to God? If God is all-powerful, he should
be able to effect anything that is possible. We speak of what
is humanly possible, and presumably the phrase covers all the
things that a human can do. If God's power meant simply that
God can do all the things that God can do, this would not capture the seeming import of calling him all-powerful or omnipotent. "If we should say that God is omnipotent because he can
do all things that are possible for him to do, there would be a
circle in our manifestation of the divine omnipotence: this would
be to say nothing more than that God is omnipotent because he
can do all the things that he can do. Therefore it remains that
God is called omnipotent because he can effect anything that is
possible without qualification."[32] Thus, something is possible
relative to a given power, for example, humanly possible, or
the possible is understood without this qualification. Now something is possible or impossible, absolutely speaking, with reference to the import of terms: possible, because the predicate is
compatible with the subject, for example, that Socrates should
sit; impossible, because the predicate is incompatible with
the subject, for example, that a man should be a donkey.

The power of an agent is read from the sort or kind of being
the agent is; things of different kinds have effects, or can perform acts, of different kinds. But God is not a restricted kind
of being; he is a being who is the fullness of being, possessing

in a unified way the perfections found separate and, as it were, scattered among the sorts or kinds of things which are his effects. The power of such a being must extend as widely as being itself, which is to say that God's power encompasses any and every being.

Nothing is opposed to the notion of being except non-being. Therefore only that will be repugnant to the notion of the absolutely possible, the object of the divine omnipotence, which simultaneously implies in itself being and non-being. *That* is not subject to the divine omnipotence, not because of any deficiency of divine power, but because it does not qualify as makeable or possible. But whatever does not involve a contradiction is contained among the possibles with respect to which God is called omnipotent. Whatever does involve a contradiction is not included in the divine omnipotence because it does not have the note of possible. That is why it is better to say *they cannot be made* than that *God cannot make them.*[33]

God can bring into existence anything that can exist, anything that can possibly be. The question of human freedom can now be restated wtih reference to the divine omnipotence.

In the first place, there is no difficulty with the notion that God can make creatures whose actions and activities follow necessarily. Thomas would not agree that every event has a cause when this is taken to mean that every event is determined by its cause or causes, but he would of course allow that some things happen necessarily.[34] Indeed, it is necessary that a man will die, so that even if we grant that man is a free agent, we are not saying that every event stemming from him is a product of his freedom. Man can abuse his freedom and bring about his own death, but he cannot choose whether or not to be mortal. The way in which freedom can be related to divine omnipotence such that it causes a most difficult problem is this: Can God create a free creature who cannot not do what he freely does? Is such a situation possible in the absolute sense just defined?

It would seem not to be. A free action is one that may or may not be performed, something the agent can do or not do. But surely it is contradictory to say of this same action that it is at once free and one that the agent cannot not do. Let us be more precise. If I take as an example of a free action my drinking this glass of water, I am not of course suggesting that, while I am drinking this glass of water, I could be not drinking this glass of water. While I am drinking this glass of water, I cannot not be drinking this glass of water. The necessity that is incompatible with my freely drinking the glass of water is that which would be involved in saying that I could not not have drunk this glass of water now. So we are referring the present act or event to the past; if the event is free, then the past does not determine or necessitate its taking place; if the past determines or necessitates its ·taking place, then it is not a free act.

For these reasons, God can not bring it about that a free action is one that could not not have been done. But to say this may appear to collide with the implications of divine omniscience.

B. The Divine Omniscience

When God is said to be omniscient, the meaning is that he knows not only everything that actually is but also everything that it is in his power or in that of any of his creatures to do.[35] That means that he knows what will happen in the future, future contingent events. Some causes produce their effects necessarily, and to know such effects in their causes, before they are produced, is not the kind of knowledge of what will happen that interests us here. Rather, we are thinking of future events due to causes which could possibly not produce or bring about the events in question. Is it possible for anyone to have certain knowledge of future events of that kind, as future, before they happen? We might have conjectural, probable knowledge of such events. To another we might say, though it is usually inadvisable to do so, "I knew you were going to do that." And there might have been high probability in our antecedent prediction; but we could not have been certain in the sense that we knew the other could not not do what he went on to do. God, on the other hand, in the view of St. Thomas, knows all contingent events, not only as they are in their causes, but also as each of them actually is in itself.

Although contingent events come actually to be successively, God does not know them successively, the way they take place, as we do, but all at once. The reason is that his knowledge is measured by eternity, as is his existence, and eternity being total and simultaneous being encompasses the whole of time. . . . Hence whatever is in time is eternally present to God.[36]

Future contingents are not future to God. He sees them as if they were all happening now. But what he sees to be happening cannot not be happening. Among the future contingents which he sees and which thus cannot not be happening are human free acts. Is that a contradiction?

If God knows this will be, it will be. If God knows what is going to happen, it happens necessarily.

But those things which are known by God are necessary according to the mode whereby they come under the divine knowledge, and not absolutely, as considered in their proximate causes. Hence this proposition, "Whatever is known by God necessarily is," is customarily distinguished: that is, it can be understood either *de re* or *de dicto*. If it is understood *de re*, of the thing he knows, it is divided and it is false, for its sense would be, "Everything that God knows is necessary." Understood *de dicto*, it is composite and true, for its sense is, "This dictum, that which is known by God, is necessary."[37]

It might be objected that this distinction is not applicable here. If I should say, "What is white can be black," then, admittedly, understood *de dicto*, that is, "It is possible that white is black," it is false, while understood *de re*, that is, "That which is white can be black," it is true. It is not possible that black is white; but that which is white could be black. Here the distinction works because the forms or qualities are distinguishable from a subject having them. But, "A blackbird can be white" is false, whether the possibility be understood *de re* or *de dicto*, of what is being talked about or the way of talking about it, because black is not a quality the blackbird can fail to have. But is not to be known by God somewhat like the blackness of the blackbird? What is known by God cannot not be known by God.

To this, Thomas replies that "to be known" is not an inherent quality of the thing known in the way that black is of the blackbird. Rather, "to be known" refers to the act of the knower, and that is why something can be attributed to the thing known in itself, though it is always known, which is not attributed to it insofar as it is an object of knowledge. To be material is attributed to a rock as it exists, but it is not attributed to it as it is known.[38]

Difficult matters, these, and what we have said of them perhaps generates as much obscurity as it dissipates. The point would seem to be that the necessity which qualifies God's knowledge does not spill over into the things he knows, such that they in themselves are necessary. This means that if God knows a future free act as if it were present, his knowledge cannot fail to be true, it is necessarily true; nonetheless, the free act he knows necessarily, as it occurs, in itself, remains free. So we are not confronted with a contradiction. No free act is in itself a necessary occurrence, even though God's eternal knowledge, seeing it as present, cannot be false, is necessarily true. And this, as it happens, is roughly what we find in Boethius, both in the *Consolation of Philosophy*, Books Four and Five, and in his commentary on Aristotle's *On Interpretation* to which Thomas makes reference in his own commentary.[39]

CHAPTER 4

Thomas Aquinas and Platonism

I *The Platonism of the Fathers*

THE acceptance of Aristotle as *the* philosopher carries with it an attitude toward Plato. However reluctant he may have been to criticize his mentor and other old friends, Aristotle managed to conquer his disinclination frequently enough to leave us a picture of Platonism that is not calculated to win adherents to the teachings of his old master. It is not an ideal situation for a philosophical doctrine to be both described and assessed by an adversary. We ourselves can test the accuracy of Aristotle's account of what Plato said by turning to Plato himself, but, as we have observed, this course was not open to Thomas Aquinas. There simply was not that much Plato in Latin translation. The *Timaeus*, a partial translation of which had been available for some time, is not, one might say, the most typical Platonic dialogue. It *may* be that Thomas saw translations of the *Meno* and *Phaedo*, but we do not know this for certain. Clearly then, from the point of view of the writings of the two philosophers, Thomas was in the position of having all or most of Aristotle and next to none of Plato. From this we might want to conclude that things would surely have been different if Thomas had been able to turn that brilliant and sympathetic mind of his onto the Dialogues. Could he have failed to respond to the sinuous intellectual excitement of the *Theaetetus* or *Sophist*, and would he not have found the *Parmenides* a metaphysical feast of the first order? What a shame, this vision of a past contrary to fact concludes, that the battle for Thomas's mind was such an unequal one.

There are not wanting scholars to contend that Plato, despite the unevenness of the match, came close to winning the mind of Thomas.[1] Within the massive figure of that Italian friar, we are urged to believe, there was a Platonist struggling to get out. Nor was this merely the *genius loci* at work, the spirit of Greek philosophy haunting still the southern parts of Italy. We need not rely on thoughts of Plato's trips to Sicily, building from them and from Thomas's birthplace the notion that the two men were, in a way, fellow citizens. The fact is that from the point of view of influence, from Patristic times on into the 13th century, the balance was tipped in favor of Plato.

Influence is a far more subtle thing than the factual givenness of the texts of an author, but it is nonetheless a factor and one that can be traced with reasonable accuracy. It is by way of being a cliché that the pagan philosopher whom the Fathers of the Church found most congenial was Plato.[2] If they found any good at all in philosophy, it was because of Plato. Indeed, so compatible did they find him that they professed to see foreshadowings of Christian doctrine in his writings. Or was it that they saw the tenets of the faith through the medium of Platonism? Certainly some of the Fathers studied philosophy before becoming Christians. The study of philosophy in the early centuries of our era went on in a situation almost the exact reverse of the one we find in the 13th century. If in the latter, it is Aristotle who can be read and Plato who is lost, in the former Plato is read, the Academy continues, while Aristotle is lost. This phenomenon of the lost Aristotle fascinates scholars.[3] Stories were told of how the loss occurred: texts buried, only to be discovered later. Yet in one way Aristotle was not lost. Cicero, who studied in Athens, remarks on the beauty of Aristotle's style, a judgment which is bound to give pause to the student of the Treatises but which, given the stature of Cicero, can scarcely be dismissed out of hand. What is the explanation? It seems to be this. Besides the Treatises, which for us *are* Aristotle, namely, the *Physics, On the Soul, Metaphysics, Politics, Nicomachean Ethics*, and so forth, Aristotle also wrote dialogues. It is the dialogues that Cicero must have had in mind, and we wonder if he knew the Treatises. Perhaps not.

Lest we think that all this has been resolved in our times, consider this final ironic twist. As soon as Aristotle comes into the West in force, in the Treatises, his dialogues drop out of sight. To this very day, scholars are piecing together those lost writings of Aristotle. What we have of them produces a surprising effect. We have been instructed, by Aristotle himself in the Treatises, to regard his thought as in the main opposed to that of Plato. But in the dialogues, as they have been reconstructed, it is a Platonic Aristotle we read—in themes, in style, even in doctrine. It was this which underlay the theory of Werner Jaeger that we shall allude to in our next chapter. And how do scholars reconstruct a lost text? By searching in Hellenistic and Patristic writers for allusions, paraphrases, direct quotations. When any of the Church Fathers mentions Aristotle with approval, chances are that he is thinking of a dialogue rather than of a treatise.

All this is important because the Church Fathers are important. Their influence on theology and philosophy throughout the Middle Ages was enormous. After Scripture, they constitute the chief authority and guide for the interpretation of the mysteries of faith. Thus, if they were as a group largely Platonist in outlook, the influence of Plato on the Middle Ages can hardly be discounted. In the previous chapter, in discussing two quite different accounts of the division of theoretical science in the works of Boethius, we suggested that he reveals a Platonic predilection. But the single greatest vehicle of Platonic influence was Saint Augustine.

A. Saint Augustine (345–430)

The whole matter of Augustine's relationship to Platonism is vexed and complicated. If we try to give a fairly straightforward account here, we nevertheless remind the reader that there are difficulties we are not taking into account, although, of course, none of them is thought to falsify the picture we sketch. In the *Confessions*, Augustine tells us that he studied Greek but that it did not take. There is therefore reason to doubt that he ever read Plato, and the linguistic problem remains for one who would say that the real influence on Augustine was not Plato but the Neoplatonist Plotinus. Add to this the fact that Augustine wrote a book of some length entitled *Contra academicos*, that is, against the members of Plato's

Academy. The point is that (a) there are problems of access to Plato, and indeed to Plotinus, if Augustine did not read Greek, and (b) there is a prima facie case that, whatever the manner of his acquisition of knowledge about it, his assessment of Platonism was negative.

It is very easy, however, to construct an opposed picture in which Augustine appears excessively laudatory of Platonism. Indeed, in the very work he wrote against the members of the Academy, Augustine calls Plato "the wisest and most learned man of his time,"[4] and the passage continues as a veritable paean of praise. Plato has achieved the perfect philosophy, one that Augustine regards as all but indistinguishable from Christianity. The fact that Plato's principal concerns were God and the soul was bound to commend him to Augustine, and, in *The City of God*,[5] he tells us that Plato taught that God is incorporeal, immutable, surpassing every soul, cause of all else, understanding and happiness. In the same work,[6] Augustine holds that happiness is the aim of philosophy. Consequently, if God is happiness, it would seem that the aim of philosophy is to attain to God.

There are difficulties in the way of the Christian who sees pagans engaged in a pursuit whose aim is union with God. St. Paul warned believers not to be led astray by philosophy (Col. 2:8). Augustine quotes the passage, but balances it with what Paul wrote to the Romans (Rom. 1:19–20). The message would seem to be one of caution, and Augustine feels that it cannot be philosophers like the Platonists against whom Paul warned. "This, therefore, is the reason why we prefer these to all the others, because, while other philosophers have worn out their minds and powers in seeking the causes of things, and in endeavoring to discover the right mode of learning and living, these, by knowing God, have found where resides the cause by which the universe has been constituted, and the light by which truth is to be discovered, and the fountain at which felicity is to be drunk."[7]

We can trace in the writings of Augustine alterations in his attitude toward Platonism. As a line, it would start at the left, high on the chart of approval, and then gradually descend as it proceeds, but always staying on the chart and far from the bottom. Along this line, we find Augustine toying with the idea that the *Timaeus* was influenced by Genesis. The Platonists almost but not quite taught the doctrine of the Trinity. He sees few obstacles in the way of concordance: "Now in the matter of authority, I have chosen Christ for my leader, from whose direction I will never deviate.... As regards the matters which are to be investigated by close reasoning, I am such that I impatiently desire to grasp the truth not only through faith but also through understanding, and I am confident that there will be found in the Platonists nothing repugnant to faith."[8] His ardor may cool, but for Augustine Plato remains *the* philosopher.

What is the main attraction that Platonism holds for Augustine? Precisely what, in reading Aristotle, we would take to be the central tenet of Platonism, namely, the Ideas. "... Plato thought there were two worlds, one intelligible, another manifest to us by sight and touch. The former is the principle of pure and serene truth in the soul which knows itself, whereas the latter can engender opinion in the minds of the foolish but not science."[9] Augustine goes on: "The Ideas are the chief forms or the stable and unchangeable notions of things which have not themselves been formed and thus are eternal and unalterable; they are contained in the divine intelligence."[10] The Ideas thus play a dual role: (a) epistemologically, they provide adequate objects for intellectual knowing: they are stable, unchanging, immaterial; (b) ontologically, they are the patterns, types, and, at least in that sense, the causes of physical things. The place of these Ideas is the divine intelligence; they are not a realm of things distinct from God. Indeed, they are identifiable with the Divine Word, the Second Person of the Trinity. They are the patterns according to which God created.

We shall be interested in what Thomas makes of this. What has he to say of the Ideas? What has he to say of the theory of knowledge attached to the doctrine of Ideas? If we can get some clarity on these two matters, we shall know a good deal of what Thomas thought of the Platonism of Augustine.

B. Pseudo-Dionysius

When we hear that the author most quoted by Thomas in the *Summa theologiae* is Pseudo-Dionysius, we can be forgiven our surprise.[11] Scholars may know him, but this Dionysius, or Denis, is hardly a household name. Indeed, precisely who he was is lost in obscurity, an obscurity he deliberately fostered by describing himself as that Denis the Areopagite converted by St. Paul. Since his works could not have been written much before A.D. 500, we must either grant him the lifespan of an Old Testament patriarch or doubt his word. He is called the Pseudo-Dionysius. But Thomas Aquinas had no reason to doubt the apostolic connections of Denis and thus he treats him with the deference due texts that are the next thing to the canonical writings themselves. Those writings, èven when we are forced to recognize that their author was putting on the act of an apostle, bear close reading. Thomas clearly knew them well. They are: *On the Celestial Hierarchy, On the Ecclesiastical Hierarchy, On the Divine Names,* and *On Mystical Theology.* Thomas wrote a commentary on the work on the divine names, and it is a marvel of profundity and subtlety. Here, as in the *Book of Causes,* compiled as we have seen from the Neoplatonist Proclus's *Elements of Theology,* Thomas must confront that corrolary to the doctrine of Ideas, namely, participation. Aristotle singled out participation for obloquy. Nonetheless, as several scholars have shown,[12] participation is not something that Thomas rejects as Aristotle did.

We have, then, a number of points consideration of which will give us some insight into Thomas's attitude toward Platonism. The first has to do with Ideas, their cognitive and ontological role. The second has to do with participation. We shall discuss the first in terms of the problem of universals and of the theory of knowledge. We shall discuss the second with especial reference to the names of God.

II   *The Problem of Universals*

The problem of universals was bequeathed to the Middle Ages by Boethius in his translation of and commentary on the *Isagoge* of Porphyry.[13] Porphyry was writing an introduction to the *Categories* of Aristotle in which the supreme genera of things are discussed. In the genus of substance, we might say, fall the various elements which enter into the definitions of species of substance. We are, in short, face to face with the topic on which Plato and Aristotle diverge, a topic which Porphyry tells his reader is too abstruse to be discussed in an introductory work. However, he goes on to enumerate the components of the disagreement he will not discuss. The problem of universals turns out to be three questions that can be asked about the status of genera and species. Before listing those questions, we should have in mind the definitions of "genus" and "species" that Porphyry provides. A genus is predicable of many specifically different things, as living body is predicable of plants and beasts. A species is predicable of many numerically different things, as man is predicable of Socrates and Plato. Now of genera and species we can ask: (1) Do they subsist, or are they only aspects or products of our understanding of subsistent things? (2) If they subsist, are they corporeal or incorporeal? (3) If incorporeal, where are they, separate from sensible things or located in them?

The very development of the questions has a Platonic flavor. It is as if we asked whether, in a list of the things that are, we must include, over and above entities like Socrates and Plato, man, animal, and substance. The second question is phrased on the assumption that genera and species are subsistent things. Given that, we are meant to inquire whether they are bodily or not. And then, apparently assuming that they are incorporeal, the third question asks after the location of them, apart from or somehow within corporeal things.

It may be read as an Aristotelian parody of Platonism, but the simplest way of stating the doctrine of Ideas is to say that for Plato a term that is a common name of physical objects is the proper name of another kind of object, a separate incorporeal entity. Thus, if "man" is a common noun with respect to Plato and Socrates, it is the proper name of an entity, Man, Manhood, or Humanity, by participation in which individuals are and are what they are. Thus, solutions to the problem of universals can be thought of as theories of the meanings of common nouns. The motive for thinking that there must be separate objects which respond to common nouns considered as proper names is clear.

Let us say that I have vast knowledge of fruit flies. You ask me what a fruit fly is and what a fruit fly does and I answer with that pithy clarity one expects of experts. "But which fruit fly are you speaking of?" you ask. A tolerant grimace disfigures my normally pleasant countenance. I explain that I am not speaking of any particular fruit fly. The complete present population of fruit flies could be replaced by different fruit flies and what I have told you will continue to obtain. My knowledge of fruit flies is not something that ceases to be when one or indeed the whole set of existent fruit flies ceases to be. But what do I, know if the object of my knowledge is not these particular fruit flies? Quite spontaneously, perhaps, we want to say that what the entomologist knows is the nature of fruit flies, fruit-flyness, as it were. And what is that? Where is it? These are the questions which make up the problem of universals. The Platonic answer was the doctrine of Ideas, that being the term to designate the things whose proper name the common noun is. Aristotle rejected this and so did Thomas Aquinas.

Thomas writes: "The human intellect knows in a manner midway between that of sense and angelic knowing: it is not the act of any organ, but it is the power of a soul which is the form of a body, as has been seen above. Therefore, it is proper to it to know a form which exists indeed individually in corporeal matter, but not as it is in such matter. But to know that which exists in individual matter, though not as it exists in such matter, is to abstract the form from individual matter, which sense images represent. Therefore, we must say that our intellect understands material things by abstracting from sense images; and it is by means of material things thus understood that we come to some knowledge of immaterial things, whereas for angels the reverse is true."[14] A way of getting at what Thomas is saying here is the following. Consider this sequence:

(1)   Man is a species.
(2)   Socrates is a man.
(3)   Socrates is a species.

This is unacceptable. To see why, we need only recall the meaning of "species." Something is said to be a species insofar as it is predicable of many numerically different things. Socrates cannot be predicated of numerically different things. But the following sequence is all right:

(4) Man is capable of laughter.
(5) Socrates is man.
(6) Socrates is capable of laughter.

The capacity to laugh pertains to human nature as it is found in individuals like Socrates, whereas predicability-of-many, that is, universality, does not. Nonetheless, the capacity to laugh does not pertain to human nature as it is found in individuals in the way in which running does. That is,

(7) Socrates is running

is true, let us say, and this can be expressed as

(8) Man is running.

But we cannot continue thus:

(9) Plato is a man.
(10) Plato is running.

Thus, something pertains to, is predicated of, a nature in different ways. Thomas therefore notes that nature or essence can be considered in two ways.

In one way according to its proper notion, and this is an absolute consideration of it, and thus nothing is true of it which does not pertain to it as such; to attribute anything else to it is false. For example, rational and animal and whatever enters into his definition pertains to man as man, whereas white or black or whatever is not of the definition of man does not pertain to man as man. That is why, if we are asked if this nature is one or many, we should not concede that it is either, because both are outside the concept of humanity and both can pertain to it only accidentally.[15]

If plurality belonged to human nature as such, it could not be one, as it is in Socrates; if uniqueness belonged to it as such, it could not be multiplied in Socrates, Plato, and so on.

In another way the nature can be considered as it is had by this or that, and thus something can be predicated of it accidentally, by reason of the subject which has it, as we say that man is white because Socrates is white, although this does not pertain to man as such.[16]

In (4) above, we have an instance of something said of human nature as such. What is the basis of (1) and (8)?

This nature, however, has a twofold existence: one in singulars and another in the soul, and following on either things can be said accidentally of the nature; in singulars, it has as well a multiple existence because of their diversity. Neither of these pertains to the nature considered in the first way, the absolute consideration of it. For it is false to say that the essence of man, as man, has existence in this singular, since if existence in this singular pertained to man as man, the nature could only be in this singular; by the same token, if not to be in this singular pertained to man as man, the nature would never be in it.[17]

Something can be true of human nature *as it exists in the mind* or *as it exists in singulars* that is not true of it as such. Now one of the things which pertains to human nature as a consequence or concomitant of our way of knowing it is precisely universality: predicability of many. That is why our sequence (1)–(3) did not work; it commits the fallacy of the *per accidens*.

Thomas's solution to the problem of universals, then, is this. To-be-a-species or to-be-a-genus is true of the nature *per accidens* because of our mode of knowing the forms or natures of material things. The nature as considered by us does not therefore warrant the claim that there must be additional subsistent things, out there, things like Plato's Ideas.

But what of Thomas and Augustine? Surely when Augustine speaks of the Ideas, he has something different in mind from what Plato meant by the term. For Augustine, the Ideas are patterns in the divine mind according to which God creates. Thomas has little difficulty accepting this Augustinian relocation of the Ideas. We must, he says, posit Ideas in the divine mind.[18] *Idea* can be rendered in Latin as *forma*, and by Ideas can be understood the forms of other things existing apart from those things. But the form of a thing existing apart from it can be one of two things, insofar as its exemplar is said to be its form, or as the principle of knowing it is, for the forms of knowable things are said to be in the knower. In both understandings of the term, he concludes, we must posit Ideas.

In anything that does not come about simply by chance, the form is the end of the generation. But an agent does not act for the sake of a form unless it has a similitude of the form in itself, something which can obtain in two ways. In some agents, the form of the thing to be made preexists according to natural existence, as in things which act through nature: thus man generates man and fire fire. In other agents, however, it has an intelligible existence: thus the similitude of the house preexists in the mind of the builder. And this can be called the Idea of the house: since the builder means the house to be like the form he has mentally conceived.[19]

Even the example is Augustinian. And the application is clear. The world did not come about due to chance, but was made by God. God needed then to have in mind a form to the likeness of which the world was made. And this is the sense of *Idea*.

So we see Thomas rejecting Platonic Ideas insofar as these are invoked to solve the problem of universals and instead opting for the Aristotelian solution. Nonetheless, he is able to accept what Augustine has made of the Ideas, namely, the patterns according to which God creates. But there are difficulties with, and divergences from, the Augustinian position insofar as Ideas are invoked to speak not of God's creative knowing but of ordinary human knowing.

III   *Illumination and Abstraction*

One of the motivations for the development of the Platonic doctrine of Ideas is to be found in the origin of knowledge. Earlier, we portrayed it largely in terms of the commensurate object of knowledge: singulars as such do not seem to explain knowledge; therefore, let us introduce another realm of entities that will. But then the question arises, and of course it arose for Plato too: what is the mode of our access to the Ideas? However fraught with imperfection the evanescent things of the physical world may be, and however precarious our cognitive grasp of them, that we are cognitively in contact with them, in some way, does not seem terribly problematic. But if knowledge in the strong sense bears on another realm of entities, how do we get into contact with them? In perception, the fact that we *see* things is just that, a fact, a starting point, however it is to be explained. Can we say that in some similarly direct and immediate way we *see* the Ideas? Plato grappled with this in a variety of ways; he even told some stories that were meant to circumvent the difficulty. Thus, he suggested that the soul existed prior to its union with the body, in which state it was on intimate terms with the things that really are, the Ideas. Then, presumably, the eye of the soul simply saw them. Well, something happened.

Imagine such a soul plunged into a body, imprisoned there, and say that now the eye of the soul is darkened because it is tempted to think that the things it sees through the bodily eye are real. And this of course is a delusion. Who can read the passage in the *Republic* where Plato likens us to prisoners in a cave, condemned to face the back wall upon which the shadows of artifacts are cast by a fire behind us, without being profoundly moved? The task of philosophy, of those moved by the love of wisdom, is to free us from such delusion. The things of this world may function to remind us of the really real things, the Ideas, whose pale imitations they are; then the mind and soul can turn away from the world of change and return to the realm of Ideas.

This dramatic portrait of the human situation had a deserved impact on the Church Fathers, as it must perhaps on anyone: the idea of man as an exiled soul, of this life as a time of trial during which one could earn the right to return to a lost and better condition, and of the tugging of our attention away from the evanescent things of this world toward the Ideas, the eternal, the divine. Can we wonder that Augustine found this vision attractive and in many ways an adumbration of Christianity? Yet his acceptance of it led him inevitably in the direction of the unacceptable.

The Ideas, we remember, function as the objects of true knowledge. Any true knowledge. But Augustine has identified the Ideas with the Divine Ideas and finally with the Word of God. Does he mean to say that, whenever we know, really know, we are somehow knowing the Divine Ideas, knowing God? Like Plato, he does not see how the changing, contingent things of this world can explain necessary unchanging knowledge. The Augustinians of Thomas's own time took this to mean that Aristotle's account of intellectual knowledge, by way of abstraction from sense images, would not do.[20] There might be a role, a subsidiary role, for abstraction. But knowledge in any truly serious sense of the term requires illumination, a direct imparting from God, a participation in the kind of knowledge God has of the Ideas. Thomas confronts this implication directly and with explicit reference to Augustine.

Augustine, he notes,[21] imbued as he was with Platonism, tended to accept from it everything compatible with the faith and to alter that which was incompatible in such a way that it became acceptable. Now Plato held, as we have seen, that the forms of things subsist in themselves apart from matter, and he called these forms Ideas. It was by participation in these Ideas that our minds know whatever they know. Corporeal matter, by participation in the Idea of stone, becomes a stone, and so too, by participation in the same Idea, our minds know stone.

But because it seems alien to faith to hold that the forms of things subsist in themselves without matter, as the Platonists held, saying that Life Itself and Wisdom Itself are creative substances, as Denis had in *On the Divine Names,* Chapter 11, Augustine in the *83 Diverse Questions,* Question 46, put in place of the Ideas Plato posited notions of all things existing in the divine mind, according to which all things are fashioned and according to which also the human soul knows all things.[22]

Now, when it is asked whether the human soul knows all things in the eternal Ideas, we should reply that something can be known in another thing in two ways.

In one way, as in the object known, as one sees in a mirror those things whose images are reflected there. In this way, in the present life, we cannot see things in the eternal notions, but this is the way the blessed know who see God and all things in God. In another way, something is said to be known in something as in the principle of the knowledge: as we say that things are seen in the sun which are seen in the light of the sun. It is thus that we must say that the human soul knows all things in the eternal notions, through participation in which we know all things. But the intellectual light which is in us is nothing other than a participated similitude of uncreated light, in which are constituted the eternal notions.[23]

Perhaps the most intricate Augustinian treatment of this matter is to be found in his dialogue *On the Teacher,* which is by way of being an extended gloss on the text that we have no other teacher but Christ, who teaches within. Thomas, in his *Disputed Question On the Teacher,*[24] shows himself at his synthesizing best when he effectively identifies the participated created light in our soul, thanks to which we know what we know, with Aristotle's agent intellect, which is a faculty of the soul.

IV   *Essential and Participated Perfection*

Thus far, we have seen Thomas confront two aspects of Platonism in a manner which suggests that Platonic doctrines receive their *laissez-passer* only if they can be construed in an Aristotelian fashion. Scholars who profess to see Thomas vacillate between Aristotle and Plato, and even to opt for the latter over the former, must overlook some rather striking evidence to the contrary. The commentary on the *Book of Causes,* in its entirety, exhibits a Thomas for whom Platonism must always justify itself at the bar of Aristotelianism. This cannot be dismissed as simply a terminological matter, as if he were helping his reader with a difficult text by recasting its message in a more familiar vocabulary. His procedure is clearly judgmental.[25] When he rejects things, it is not simply because Proclus says something different from Aristotle, but because the difference involves him in falsity.

There are, it is true, times when Thomas suggests that Plato has it over Aristotle. One instance of this may be found in the *Treatise on Separated Substances,* where he seems to commend Plato for not restricting the number of separated substances, or angels, to the number of celestial movements, as Aristotle did.[26] Nonetheless, later in the same work,[27] he refutes the Platonic doctrine of Ideas. It is as if he feels that Aristotle gives a rational justification for holding that there are immaterial, separate substances, but that the very mode of his proof limits him in the number he can justify. If we could only waive the fact that Plato's talk about separate substances is not justified, based as it is upon a mistake about common nouns, it would be preferable to have the vast number of them that he speaks of.

Now if there is anywhere that we would expect an alleged wavering on the question of Platonism and Aristotelianism to exhibit itself, it would be when Thomas comments on the work of Pseudo-Dionysius. For Thomas, as we have noted, this author was Denis the Areopagite, a man who had known St. Paul and had indeed been converted by him. Far more than in the case of Augustine even, Thomas would have been reluctant to be critical here of an undeniable Platonism. But does he waver? He does not. In the proemium to his commentary, he gives a sketch of the Platonic doctrine of Ideas, and then says this: "This argument of the Platonists, then, is consonant neither with faith nor with the truth in regard to what it says about separated natural species, but in regard to what it says about the first principle of all things, their opinion is most true and it is consonant with Christian faith."[28] It is this distinction in the possible understanding of the Platonic thing-in-itself that we want now to examine.

The Platonism Thomas rejects holds that this man, that man, the other man, singular entities all, are and are what they are by participating in the Idea of Man-itself, or humanity. Thus, to be a man is to partake of, to share in, humanity. The living thing is such because it shares in, participates in, Life-itself. And so on. We have here what Socrates calls the easy mode of explanation. Why are two numbers equal? Because they participate in equality. Why are marbles round? Because they partake of roundness. And when the abstract term, or the concrete term with "itself" added, is taken to be the proper name of a separate entity, this mode of talk, innocuous in itself, becomes Platonism. And the Platonism that Thomas rejects.

At the same time, he suggests that this sort of framework has application when we wish to speak of the first cause of things, the first principle God is. While we should hesitate to say that there is some separate entity, humanity, which is the cause of individual men, or some separate entity, whiteness, which brings it about that some things are white, this kind of talk does not seem so odd when it shows up in, "There is a separate immaterially existing being which is the cause of all beings." The beings which are the effects can be said to have, to possess, or to partake of, existence; the being who is the cause of their existing can be said to be Existence-itself. We are familiar with the tendency, when speaking of God, to use abstract terms almost in preference to concrete ones. God is being, in the sense of a being, yes, but better to say that he is existence, beingness. God is wise, and God is wisdom. God is good, and God is goodness. The model that the Platonist mistakenly applies to terms abstractly expressing the formal and inherent properties of creatures seems just what we want when we talk about God.

If we should say of a woman that she is beautiful and then, pained by the inadequacy of the remark, say that she is beauty; if we should say of someone that he is wisdom or justice personified, we would seem to be recognizing that simply to say that one is beautiful, wise, or just allows for the fact that the one we are speaking of does not exhaust the meaning of beauty, wisdom, and justice. The trouble is that beauty and wisdom and justice do not seem to be among the things that are in the same sense that beautiful, wise, and just individuals are.[29] The concrete term has the merit that its mode of signification suggests subsistence, but the defect that a limitation of the perfection by which the thing is designated is also suggested. The abstract term has the merit of expressing a perfection as unlimited, but the defect that its mode of signifying does not suggest that it can directly apply to a subsistent thing. That is why both concrete and abstract terms are inadequate when applied to God.[30] Still, there is an especial attraction in abstract terms and, though we are conscious that our language is being strained to the utmost when we do this, we want to say that God is wisdom, God is justice, God is goodness.

One of the objections to Plato is that the realm of abstract entities multiplies ferociously once we admit Ideas. From Socrates alone we generate humanity, animality, rationality, life, knowledge, substance, being, and so on. If the model employed by the generation of Ideas is to be applied to talk about God, we are going to need (a) criteria for accepting the abstract terms that can be applied to God, (b) the proviso that a multitude of abstract terms does not argue for a plurality of referents: there is only one God, and (c) a way of relating the abstract terms applicable to God to one another: is one of them least inadequate as a name of God?

If we return to an earlier example, we can distinguish between particular fruit flies and fruit-flyness: the latter will be what the former have, share in, partake of. Very well. But surely we would hesitate to think of fruit-flyness as a name of God. Why? The abstract term, unlike the concrete term, has an unrestricted mode of signifying, yet the perfection, form, or nature signified contains matter as part of its definition. Not even abstract fruit-flyness can get along without wings and senses and so forth. But such material, corporeal features, much as they are part of the perfection of fruit-flyness, are, on a cosmic scale, imperfections.

Abstract terms like justice, wisdom, and goodness fare better as names of God because not only do they escape from the restricted modes of the corresponding concrete terms—just, wise, good—but the perfection itself does not as such involve material and corporeal components.

> But again from the side of what is formal, in some of these a certain imperfection is designated; as in desire, which is of a good not had; and in sadness, which is of an evil had. The same is true of anger, which presupposes sadness. There are some, however, which designate no imperfection, like love and joy. Since then none of these belongs to God according to what is material in them . . . those which imply imperfection even when considered formally can pertain to God only metaphorically, because of some similarity of effect. . . . Those which do not imply imperfection can properly be said of God, like love and joy.[31]

The only way we can talk of God, the only way God can talk to us, is through a language devised to speak of quite different sorts of things. It is in knowing these things that we can come to knowledge of their cause, and the cause is thus spoken of, designated, from his effects. What Thomas is giving above are criteria for selecting the effects whose names can be transferred to God.

If wisdom and justice and goodness are names of God and God is absolutely one and simple,[32] are these terms synonymous? Thomas thinks not.[33] They all, all the names of God, have the same referent, but they have different senses or meanings. It is when we find a created perfection which, while limited in creatures, does not, considered abstractly, seem to demand the restricted created mode, that we have a way of talking about God. And of course each of them is inadequate to express what God is. We can fashion a notion of unrestricted goodness by negating the limitations of created good things, but this does not enable us to understand what it would be like for goodness itself to exist. These abstract terms, drawn as they are from distinct perfections, retain their different senses. A further mark of their inadequacy is that we cannot understand how the referent of justice, mercy, and love, say, can be an utterly simple entity.

For the Neoplatonist, for Pseudo-Dionysius,[34] such abstract terms, considered as names of God, relate to one another in the following way: there is a hierarchy or order among them with being or existence first, then life, then wisdom, and so on. Let us consider just these three. The point about Aristotle's objection to the proliferation of Ideas is that, in reifying genera and species and thereby establishing an order of subsistent imma- terial entities, a premium is put on the most abstract. The genus is more general or universal than the species, and the higher the genus the more universal it is. But the hierarchy of genera and species is, for Aristotle, a mark of the imperfection of our knowing and certainly not an indication of an objective order of more and more perfect entities as we rise toward greater generality.

Let us put the point less obscurely. To know of something that it exists, that it is a being, would seem to be to know less of it than to know that it is alive; to know that it is alive is to know less of it than to know that it is an animal; to know that it is an animal is to know less than to know that it is human, and so on. When, for instance, I finally realize that I am confronted with my mother-in-law, this is to know considerably more than I did when I knew her only as a being, however nostalgic I may in this instance be for that blissful ignorance of yore. In short, the more general the knowledge, the more confused, vague, and imperfect it is. How odd then to put a premium on such gen- erality and vagueness and to speak of the highest genera not only as existent but even as more perfect existents than fully designated concrete particulars. It is this that underlies that rather wholesale rejection of Platonism that we find in Thomas when he accuses the Platonists of confusing what is first in our knowledge with what is first in reality, of confusing the conceptual and real hierarchies.[35]

Although Thomas never wavers—how could he?—in his rejection of Platonism so understood, he nonetheless feels, as in the passage we quoted from the proemium of his commentary on Pseudo-Dionysius's *On the Divine Names,* that, with modifications, a hierarchy based on ever greater predicable universality can be used to introduce order into the various names of God. He wants to say that being itself is more perfect than life, and life than wisdom, and that Subsisting Existence Itself (*ipsum esse subsistens*) is therefore the least imperfect name of God. The following passage helps us to see what he does, as well as what he does not, mean.

Dionysius says that although existence itself (*ipsum esse*) is more perfect than life, and life itself than wisdom, if they are considered as they are distinguished by reason, nonetheless the living thing is more perfect than that which is only a being, because a living thing is also a being; and he who is wise is a being and a living being. Therefore, although being does not include in itself living and wise, because it is not necessary that whatever participates in existence participate in it according to every mode of existing, nonetheless God's very existence includes in itself life and wisdom, because none of the perfections of existence can be lacking in that which is subsisting existence itself (*ipsum esse subsistens*).[36]

Thus, who calls God existence, implies that he is wise and living, whereas, from the point of view of concrete terms, it is in calling someone wise that we imply that he is living and a being. The reversal of hierarchies, of implications, thus seems to rely on a switch from abstract to concrete terms, or vice versa. But this need not be the case. Sometimes Thomas will say that being itself (*ens commune*) contains all perfections within it. How can the least informative, the most impoverished term, become the richest and most informative one?

One way of understanding this is suggested by Thomas in his commentary on Boethius.[37] Consider the following as the formal structure of judgment:

(1)   S is P.

This form of assertion comes down to saying that something that is of such and such a kind has such and such a quality. That is, it is as if both the subject term and the predicate term function as modifications or restrictions on the assertion of existence. To be is to be something or other; to be is to be in such or such a way. It is when *ways of being* (*modi essendi*) are looked upon as restrictions on existence, on the infinitive form of the copula, is, *esse*, that, as the term "infinitive" suggests, *esse* is taken to mean existence itself, unrestricted existence, the fullness of existence. Then the subject and predicate terms suggest (a) a restriction of being and (b) a perfection that is in some way already included in *esse*. *Esse* thus becomes a sort of dialectical limit, and if we imagine all the terms that can function as subject and predicate terms—though with the restrictions mentioned earlier when we spoke of criteria of selecting divine names—collapsing into the copula, as it were, then we see what Thomas means by saying that *esse commune* or *ens commune* is the best, in the sense of the least inadequate, name of God.[38]

But the truth of the matter is that the first cause is above being insofar as it is infinite existence itself. Being suggests that which finitely participates in existence, and this is what is proportionate to our intellect, whose object is that which is, as is said in *On the Soul*, Book Three. Hence, that alone is graspable by our intellect which has a whatness participating in existence. But the whatness of God is existence itself and thus he is above understanding.[39]

The names of God, fashioned as they are from terms devised to speak of creatures, enable us to make true statements about God but not to know *what* the God of whom we speak truly is.[40] This sounds paradoxical, it is paradoxical, but it is only a repetition of the point that we do not know the way or the how of the subsisting perfection God is. There is an ineradicable negative note in our knowledge of God. Our knowledge of God depends on what we know of things that need not have been, ourselves among them, yet the God we come to know is a necessary being, one whose existence is independent of his creation. These and other considerations lie behind the almost despairing confession of inadequacy involved in saying that God is being itself.

If we say that God is *esse* alone, we need not fall into the error of those who say that God is that universal existence whereby everything formally is. The being God is has this condition that nothing could be added to it. Hence by its very purity it is an *esse* distinct from all others, just as if there were a separately existing color it would differ by the very fact of its separation from a color which did not exist separately. That is why, in the development of the 9th Proposition in the *Book of Causes*, we read that the individuation of the first cause which is existence alone is due to its pure goodness. Common being (*esse commune*), however, just as it does not include addition in its understanding, does not exclude it either, for if that were the case nothing could be understood to be in which something more than being were understood. Similarly, even though he is common being, God need not lack other perfections and nobilities. Indeed God has the perfections which are in all the genera, because he is said to be perfect without measure . . . but he has them in a more excellent way than other things, because in him they are one while in others they are diverse.[41]

From first to last, then, Thomas is aware that "being," apart from the kind of consideration he is proposing, is the least informative term of all. The suggestion that by expressing no determinate mode of being, "being" somehow includes them all suggests another sense for the term. And it is another sense. As in the passage just quoted, Thomas is careful to distinguish the two senses lest we think that in calling something a being, we are thereby predicating God of it.

V *Magis Amicus Veritas*

Once, when criticizing Plato and professing his reluctance to do so, Aristotle says that while Plato is a friend, truth is a dearer one. It would be wrong to regard Thomas's attitude toward Plato, or toward Aristotle, as due to some unexamined predilection or antipathy. If he tends to be generally favorable toward Aristotle, this is the result of an assessment of the arguments Aristotle offers for the positions he maintains. Like Augustine before him, Thomas, we can imagine, saw an affinity between the separate world of Ideas and the implication of the Christian vocation that we not store up treasure in this world. So far as predilections go, we might expect him to favor Plato. He finds Aristotle's realm of separated beings to be an impoverished one, too sparsely populated. But it has the incalculable advantage that arguments of a sound sort are offered for the existence of such separate substances. And that, finally, is what counts philosophically. Of course Thomas's attitude toward both Greek philosophers is guided by his faith. Something that contradicts faith has got to be false. Needless to say, this conviction does not itself amount to a disproof of the offending philosophical claim. But this, along with many other things, will be taken up in the following chapter.

CHAPTER 5

The Tasks of Theology

S AINT, priest, friar, theologian—it is impossible to think of
Thomas Aquinas's life as other than a long and constant
meditation on the question he is said to have asked as a child,
"What is God?" Meditating on the Scriptures, reading the
Fathers, returning again and again to theological accounts of
the mysteries of faith, his writing and teaching an integral part
of his spiritual life, his effort to become what God wished him
to be—all the activities of his life coalesce and become his
response to the divine vocation. If we think his style stark and
almost shockingly matter-of-fact as he discusses the Trinity,
Incarnation, sacraments, and so forth, we may be reassured
to learn that his study and writing were punctuated by pauses
for prayer, tearful pleas for light. There are accounts of visions,
of mystical experiences, of visitations from the authors of the
scriptural books he sought to understand. When he was asked,
by letter, for his views on various questions, sometimes lists
of dozens of difficulties, he responded quickly, briefly, gladly.
His life seems one of disponibility: to God, to his religious
vocation, to his duties as a theologian. And the theologian, as
the term suggests, is forever pondering about God. In this
chapter, we shall be looking at Thomas's teaching on what and
how we can have a knowledge of, a science of, God.

We are bound to wonder why a man who believed that God
has revealed himself in Christ, that Scripture and tradition
convey God to us in a special way, that grace and the sacraments enable us to share in the divine life, should have spent
as much time as he did studying such pagan thinkers as Aristotle. What could a pre-Christian, non-Jewish thinker tell about
God that would not be exceeded by Revelation? His interest
in Aristotle cannot be explained as the fulfillment of an

127

academic duty. The fact is that few if any of his commentaries on Aristotle are the result or record of actual teaching. Furthermore, the bulk of his commentaries on Aristotle was written rather late in his career. This is not to say that Thomas lacked a motive broader than personal interest; the difficulties that heterodox interpretations of Aristotle were causing in the academic community, particularly at the University of Paris, would have been a great incentive. In other words, it could be argued that Thomas's concern with the work of Aristotle was fundamentally a theologian's interest, since he was, in effect, defending the faith against real or apparent philosophical errors. Nevertheless, and we shall be returning to this, the great point that Thomas makes is that it is possible, quite apart from religious belief, to arrive at knowledge of God. Such knowledge, he felt, had been achieved by the pagan philosophers, and the philosophical effort aimed at such knowledge is metaphysics.

I   Ontology or Theology?

In an earlier chapter, when discussing the division of theoretical philosophy into three sciences—natural science, mathematics, and metaphysics—we saw that Thomas introduced the notion of *separatio* in order to emphasize what is peculiar to metaphysics. In the context, it was clear that metaphysical considerations bear on things that are separate from matter and motion. That raises a problem, however. On the one hand, metaphysics is considered to be a wisdom, a more ranging and comprehensive science than the other particular sciences, and so, if not itself a particular science, then a general science. The concern of metaphysics is, in some sense, with everything, with whatever is. It is the conception of metaphysics as a general science that we capture by using the title ontology. On the other hand, insofar as it is said to be concerned with what exists apart from matter and motion, metaphysics would seem to be a particular science among others, having a subject matter or concern quite distinct from those of sciences like natural science and mathematics. These are not concerned with things that are separate from matter and motion. If metaphysics is concerned with this special class of things, it can be denominated from them and called theology. Which view of metaphysics is the correct one?

The question can be seen as a textual one, bearing on those books of Aristotle that are collectively called *Metaphysics*. In our own time, the conviction has grown on scholars that not only must this work be recognized as put together after Aristotle's death by a hand other than his own, it must also be seen as a pastiche, a gathering together of materials which, while they may bear some family resemblance to one another, nonetheless do not add up to a coherent unified literary work. In short, the books of the *Metaphysics* do not contain any single doctrine or science. More particularly, for the question we have raised, sometimes the books of the *Metaphysics* proceed as if metaphysics were ontology and at other times they proceed as if it were theology.[1]

Werner Jaeger, more than any other single scholar, put this problem at the center of Aristotelian studies in this century. It seemed to him that something of an evolution can be traced in the *Metaphysics* as it has come down to us. That is, in what would seem to be its earliest parts (not confined to the first books of the transmitted work), Aristotle assumes that the science beyond natural science and mathematics is concerned with things which are beyond this world, where "beyond" functions in the way it would for Plato. There are things whose existence is independent of space and time and the other conditions pertaining to the evanescent things of sense experience. Such things may be described as divine, just because their claim on existence is not menaced by change. In his early Platonic period, Jaeger suggested, Aristotle quite naturally thought of metaphysics as concerned with such transcendent, divine things *as with its subject.* As he matured intellectually and became more distinctively Aristotelian, Jaeger feels, Aristotle lost his youthful Platonic faith and doubted that there was any kind of reality other than physical objects.[2] Thus he gravitated toward the conception of metaphysics as ontology, as a general science of the acknowledged sciences, namely natural science and mathematics, whose task would be to consider the assumptions of these sciences which are too broad to fall within the scope of their own considerations. For example, both the

naturalist and the mathematician assume that it is impossible
for a thing to be and not to be at the same time and in the
same respect, or—a variation on this assumption—that the same
proposition cannot be true and false at the same time and in
the same respect. Since these assumptions are common to natural
science and to mathematics, they cannot be peculiar to either.
Such common considerations are taken up by metaphysics in
the guise of ontology, whose subject matter is being as being,
being in common, the common conditions of anything whatsoever.[3]

In one passage, as Jaeger observes, Aristotle, seemingly aware
that a statement of the three speculative sciences leaves unclear
which understanding of metaphysics is the correct one, tries
to retain both conceptions. "For one might raise the question
whether first philosophy is universal, or deals with one genus,
i.e., some kind of being." How does Aristotle answer this
question? "We answer that if there is no substance other than
those which are formed by nature, natural science will be the
first science; but if there is an immovable substance, the science
of this must be prior and must be first philosophy, and universal
in this way, because it is first. And it will belong to it to
consider being qua being—both what it is and the attributes
which belong to it qua being."[4] Whatever else may be said
of this passage, it has to be described as difficult. For Jaeger
it amounts to a sort of despairing acceptance of an impossible
amalgam: Aristotle knows it must be either/or, yet he pleads
for both/and.

We have already observed in Chapter 2 how different a
conception of the writings of Aristotle modern philology enter-
tains from that which guided such a commentator and expositor
as Aquinas. In the case in point, the *Metaphysics*, Thomas seems
to be unaware of massive literary difficulties with the text.
He was of course using a translation, indeed several translations,
and he often remarks on the differences among versions. But
as for the doctrinal tenor of which the text is the vehicle, here
Thomas sees a unified development, a coherent intellectual
effort, a single science. Already in the Proemium to his commentary, Thomas has resolved the problem that animated
Jaeger's work.[5]

Wherever many things are for the sake of the same end, it is fitting that they be directed to that end. Thus, in a political community, all are governed by one for the sake of the common good, and in the individual, the body is governed by the soul for the good of the individual. So too the many sciences which are sought for the sake of human happiness or perfection should be directed to this end by one science, which can be called wisdom, since it is the mark of the wise man that he can govern: *nam sapientis est alios ordinare.*

Such a science will be concerned with the most intelligible objects, and these can be understood in three ways. First, taking our cue from the process of learning, where certitude is gained when the causes of a given phenomenon are learned, we can say that intelligibility is a function of knowledge of causes and that the highest degree of intelligibility is had when things are known through their first, or primary, causes. Second, taking our cue from the difference between intellect and sense, we notice that the former is concerned with the universal; thus, the more universal they are, the more objects pertain to intellect and the more intelligible they will be. "By which is meant being and those things which follow on being, like one and many and potency and act. Such things ought not to be left undetermined since without knowledge of these complete knowledge of what is peculiar to a species or genus cannot be had." Thomas goes on to say that since these are common to any science, they are not appropriately treated *ex professo* by a particular science and thus should be taken up by a common science. Third, taking our cue from the nature of intellectual knowledge, namely its immateriality, we can say that those things which are most separate from matter are most intelligible. "Those things are most separate from matter which not only abstract from individual matter, like natural forms considered as universals by natural science, but from sensible matter entirely. And not only considered separately, like mathematicals, but things which exist separately, like God and the Intelligences."[6]

If wisdom or first philosophy is concerned with the most intelligible objects, that phrase turns out to be ambiguous since it covers first causes, common conditions of anything whatsoever, and God and the angels. Thus, Thomas seems to complicate the issue further by proposing three rather than only two possible subjects of metaphysics. Anticipating this bewilderment, he immediately adds that all these fall to the consideration of one science. First he identifies first causes and God and angels, that is, separate substances. That leaves us with the problem Jaeger saw. Here is Thomas's resolution of that issue.

One and the same science considers a given genus and the causes proper to that genus, just as natural science considers the principles of natural body. Thus it belongs to the same science to consider separate substances and common being, which is the genus of which the substances mentioned are the common and universal causes. From this it is clear that although this science considers the three things mentioned earlier, it does not consider each of them *as its subject*, but only common being. This is the subject of the science whose causes and properties we seek; the causes of the subject are not themselves the subject of the science.[7]

It can be seen that the only way Jaeger can have the problem he has with the *Metaphysics* is to assume that there is competition between two possible understandings of the subject of the science. That is, the suggested split between ontology and theology is interesting only if we assume that there is a distinction between subject matters involved. Unless there is a science which has, as its subject matter, separate substance, there is no possibility of the particular science Jaeger means by theology. Thomas denies that Aristotle did, or even could, propose as the subject of a science, divine being in the sense of separate substance. If a science is to consider God and separate substance, it can do so only if it has a subject matter of which God is the cause. Thus, metaphysics is a theology insofar as it is an ontology; that is, its subject matter is common being (ontology) and its concern with God (theology) is with the first cause of its subject.

However, although the subject of this science is common being, the whole of it is said to be concerned with what is separate from matter both in being and in consideration. Because it is not only those things which never exist in matter, like God and intellectual substances,

which are said to be separate from matter in being and in consideration, but also what *can* be without matter, like common being.
This would not be the case if it were dependent on matter in being.[8]

If there are some things which exist apart from matter, then
matter does not necessarily enter into the concept of being.
A thing need not be material in order to be; not every being
is a material being. It is against the background of this assumption that a science of being as being is generated.

The foregoing provides us with the way in which, for Thomas,
questions about God can enter into philosophical discourse. If
we inquire after the nature of God, we cannot pursue the
question by setting up a science the subject of which would
be God, whose nature and properties we then attempt to
discover. Why not? The main reason is accessibility. The only
way we can know of God or talk about him is indirectly,
obliquely, by analogy with something else. This dependence
of our knowledge of God on our knowledge of something else,
on his effects, as it happens, is not a temporary dependence, one
that can be ultimately dispensed with. It is permanent and
pervasive and essentially restricts the claims we can make
as to our knowledge of God. This is why theology, our knowledge of God, must be a function of our knowledge of something
else, why knowledge of God is knowledge of the cause of a
subject matter. Of course, such knowledge of God as we can
achieve is the ultimate goal of our intellectual quest. To say
that our knowledge of God is always and necessarily indirect
and analogous is not to say that it is inadvertent, unlooked for,
and accidental. Thomas would define philosophy, as a whole,
as the quest for wisdom, that is, as the quest for such knowledge
of God as is possible to natural reason.

This being said, we must now notice that there are other
difficulties concerning the determination of the subject of metaphysics. That subject is designated as being as being, *ens
commune*. 'Being,' however, is a term that has a variety of
meanings and it is not immediately clear what meaning or
meanings we are meant to have in mind. Indeed, it could be
argued that the systematic ambiguity of the term 'being' mili-
tates against its usefulness as the denominator of a subject

matter. St. Thomas, like Aristotle before him,[9] dwells on this difficulty. Aristotle had said that 'being' is said in many ways, it is an equivocal term, though it may be a deliberately equivocal one. St. Thomas will speak of it as an analogous term. Now this notion of analogous terms, terms with a controlled variety of meanings, is an extremely important one for Thomas, and it is extremely important for our purposes now. It is invoked both to argue that it is possible for there to be a determinate science of being as being and to account for the meaning of terms as they are extended from creatures to God. This indicates the procedure we must follow. First, we will give a sketch of Thomas's teaching on analogous terms or names. Then we will see how this doctrine is called into service to show that there can indeed be a science whose subject is being as being, because 'being' is an analogous term. Next we will return to the question of the nature of theology, in the course of which discussion we will see how analogy is invoked to explain how the names of God are significant.

II   *Analogous Terms*

When we talk about things, our terms are applicable to them insofar as a given account is associated with the term. For example, a given entity is called a man because the account "rational animal," say, is associated with the term 'man'. The meaning of a term may thus be either the account associated with it or the thing to which the term is applied according to that account. It is the first sense of meaning that Thomas emphasizes, though not exclusively, and it is obvious that each member of the triad is called into play no matter which meaning of meaning we have in mind. The account associated with a term (the *ratio nominis*) expresses our mental grasp of the thing. When this is a definition or when it is a description, the sorting and comparing involved in such a mental grasp is obvious.[10]

If this can suffice for present purposes, we can now understand what would be meant by saying that a number of things are spoken of univocally. Things are spoken of or named univocally when they share a common term and the same account is associated with that term. Thus Peter and Paul and Hans are all called men, each can have 'man' predicated of him, and the same account can be given each time, to wit, "rational animal." The following sort of list is therefore understood:

(1) Peter is a man.
(2) Paul is a man.
(3) Hans is a man.

Our attention is drawn to the recurrent term, the predicate of these sentences, and, in the uses assumed, we say that the term means the same thing each time. Given that, the subjects of these sentences can be called univocals as named by the same term having the same meaning.

But of course very often a recurring term does not have the same meaning in the plurality of its uses.

(4) A ball is a formal dance.
(5) A ball is a spherical toy.

What we are talking about in (4), like what we are talking about in (5), is called a ball; they share the same name, let us say. But the account we should give of what is named by *ball* in the two instances varies. Indeed, these sentences express the two different accounts and might be thought of as spelling out the different meanings of the recurrent term in:

(4') Cinderella went to the ball.

and

(5') Cousy went to the ball.

Things equivocally named share the same name, but a different account of the name is given in its various applications or uses.

It would seem to be too harsh a doctrine to say that a recurrent use of a term is such that it receives either the same account or quite different accounts in its various uses. Indeed Aristotle distinguished between what he called chance and deliberate equivocation.[11] In the former, the same term in the sense of the same vocal sound or the same orthographic symbol just happens to be associated with different meanings and no reason for the same term's being used is sought. On other occasions, it would seem that quite deliberately we use the same term, even though we would not give the same account of it. What is needed, it would seem, is something between univocation and equivocation where the latter is understood as pure or complete equivocation.[12] Deliberate equivocation is Aristotle's suggestion for that less extreme case. When things are deliberately or intentionally spoken of equivocally, they have the same name but not the same meaning nor entirely different meanings. There is some connection or relation short of identity between the various meanings associated with the deliberately or intentionally equivocal term.

(6)   Rover is healthy.
(7)   A cold nose is healthy.
(8)   Dog biscuits are healthy.

The list of sentences (6)–(8) has the recurrent term 'healthy' and we are unlikely to think that the identically same account would be given in each use and we are equally unlikely to think that the accounts given would be utterly unrelated to one another. It is this sort of situation that Thomas has in mind when he says that a term is used analogously or that things are named analogically. They share a common name with a variety of accounts which are related, which are partly the same and partly different.[13]

In order to see what this partial sameness and partial difference in the plurality of accounts associated with a term used analogously consists of, we must introduce the distinction Thomas makes between *what* a term means (*res significata*) and the *way* it means it (*modus significandi*).[14] This is a distinction within the account or *ratio nominis*. The *what* and the *way* are, as it were, components of the account. Thomas more often than not illustrates the distinction by means of abstract and concrete terms like 'white' and 'whiteness'. What these terms mean is the same, a determinate quality, but the way they mean it differs. The account of whiteness might be "that whereby white things are white" and the account of white "that which has whiteness." This suggests that the abstract term signifies in such a way that what is meant is not signified as an existent thing, but rather as a possible modification or quality of an existent thing. The concrete term, on the other hand, signifies what it signifies as existent, as a subsistent thing.

We can restate the definitions of univocals and equivocals by means of the distinction of the *what* and the *how*.[15] Thus, things are named univocally which share a name that signifies the same *what* (*res significata*) in the same way (*modus significandi*). Things are named equivocally which have a name in common but in which the *what* signified by the name is different in each case. As for analogy, things are named analogically which have the same name that signifies the same *what* (*res significata*) in each use but in a different way (*modus significandi*) in each case.

The difference between the abstract and concrete ways of signifying will not be helpful here since in our example, sentences (6)–(8), the recurrent term is concrete. What Thomas will do is to use the abstract term 'health' to stand for *what* is meant by 'healthy' in each case, and seek the variation of its meanings in the *way* it is meant. This suggests that the formal pattern for a meaning of 'healthy' is "_____ health," such that the different ways of signifying health fill in the blank and constitute a complete meaning. What are candidates for filling in the blank?[16] Thomas suggests:

a) subject of . . .
b) sign of . . .
c) preservative of . . .

To fill in the blank with (a) gives us the sense of 'healthy' needed for (6); to fill in the blank with (b) gives us the sense needed for (7); and to fill in the blank with (c) gives us the meaning of 'healthy' in (8).

We are now in possession of a clear explanation as to what is meant by a term's having a plurality of meanings which are partly the same and partly different. Their sameness consists in the fact that each meaning involves the same *what* or *res significata*, their difference in the variation of mode or *modi significandi*. But, as it happens, while this is a necessary, it is not a sufficient condition of the analogous name as Thomas understands it. One of the various ways of signifying what the term signifies takes precedence over the others. Not only is there a plurality of meanings of an analogous term, these meanings form an ordered set, they are related as prior and posterior. The primary meaning is also called by Thomas the proper meaning (*ratio propria*) of the analogous term. And he fashions the following rule: When something is said analogically of many, it is found according to its proper meaning in one of them alone.[17] Secondary meanings of the analogous term are recognized as such insofar as they presuppose the primary way of signifying what the term signifies. Thus, in the example of 'healthy', it is the meaning "subject of health" that is the *ratio propria* of the name, since the other meanings, "sign of health," for example, presuppose it because a cold nose is a sign of health in that which is a subject of health. So too, food is healthy in the sense of preservative of health in that which is the subject of health.

Needless to say, no word or term is, taken just by itself, univocal, equivocal, or analogous. "Healthy" said of Fido and Rover would be accounted a univocal term, whereas in our sentences (6)–(8), it is used analogously.

III   *Analogy and the Subject of Metaphysics*

It is this doctrine on analogous terms that enables Thomas to explain, closely following Aristotle, how it is that there can be a science of being as being. This sounds, of course, as if one were proposing a science whose concern is everything. But how could such a concern have sufficient focus for a science, given the manifest diversity of the things that are? This is what Aristotle and Aquinas are emphasizing when they say that 'being' means many things. Being is not a genus, as if to be were to be a type or sort of thing. To be is to be something or other, and there is no one kind of thing. Thus it would seem that there must be sciences of being, different sciences for different types of being, and that there cannot be a single science of being as being. This difficulty, we remember, is not handled by the previous discussion as to how the theoretical sciences differ from one another. That distinction was made in terms of the different modes of defining. But to say that metaphysics deals with things which are separate from matter both in being and consideration does not of itself tell us how such things are sufficiently one to form the subject of a single science.[18]

If the observation that 'being' has many meanings is the statement of a problem, it is also the indication of its solution insofar as we think of the way in which the analogous term has many meanings. If such a term as 'healthy' has, as an analogous term, many meanings, there is nonetheless an order among those meanings such that one of them is principal and primary and presupposed by the other meanings. Now if 'being' has many meanings in the way in which the analogous term has many meanings, then we know we are not faced with diversity pure and simple. But what sort of list are we to have in mind where being is the recurrent term that is to be interpreted as analogous?

(1)   John is human.
(2)   John is six feet tall.
(3)   John is tan.
(4)   John is seated.

Let us begin with this list. Where is the recurrent common term? 'Is'? This might be regarded as a mere copula joining predicate and subject term, and its sense might then be: the conjunction obtains or is true. For our purposes, we shall take these four sentences to say that John is in various ways; he is said to be in various ways; he exemplifies various modes of being. Thus we are interested in is-human, is-six-feet-tall, is-tan, and is-seated.

Furthermore, we can take any one of our sentences and notice that it implies other sentences.

(1)   John is human.
(1')   John is animal.
(1'')   John is alive.
(1''')   John is a substance.
(1'''') John is a being.

So too from (2), we can get:

(2)   John is six feet tall.
(2')   John has length.
(2'')   John is extended.
(2''')   John is quantified.
(2'''') John is a being.

From (3):

(3)   John is tan.
(3')   John is colored.
(3'')   John is qualified.
(3''')   John is a being.

We can see that the implications here go only in one direction.

If every human is animal, not every animal is human; if every animal is alive, not every living thing is animal; if every living thing is a substance, not every substance is living. Our generated lists of sentences go from more specific or determinate to less specific or generic designations. The most generic expression in a given line is what Aristotle and Thomas mean by a category, a supreme genus.[19] The categories express irreducible general types or ways of being and are what is had in mind when it is said that 'being' means many things or has many meanings.

Can we now apply more directly the doctrine on analogous names to this situation? We remember that the analogous name was described as one that has several meanings, each of which signifies the same *what* or *res significata* in a different *way* or *modus significandi*. What is the pattern here, in the way in which "_____ health" is the pattern for the different meanings of 'healthy' used analogously? It is: "_____ existence."[20] What are the different ways of signifying this *res significata* in the case of the categories? That which exists in itself and not in or as an aspect of another is the substantial mode of being. That for which to be is to be in another, as a modification or accident of another, is the accidental mode of being. Furthermore, this accidental mode of being presupposes the substantial mode of being, since that whose being is to be in another is, ultimately, in that which exists in itself. This latter then is the primary or principal mode of being, the *ratio propria entis*. Since this sense of 'being' is presupposed by the other and secondary senses, a science of being as being can concentrate on the principal mode of being, and that is what produces the unity of the science. The various meanings of 'being' make up an ordered set, and the science of being is chiefly and primarily concerned with that which is in the primary sense. And this is to say that the science of being as being is chiefly and primarily the science of substance.[21]

IV   *The Two Theologies*

Thus far we have seen how Thomas understands the nature of the philosophical effort to achieve knowledge of God. Let us call this conception of metaphysics philosophical theology or natural theology. Clearly what is involved here is a knowledge of God that is available to any man in principle, whether or not he is a religious believer. Indeed, the chief historical example of such natural theology would be, for Thomas, the *Metaphysics* of Aristotle. Equally clearly, Thomas maintains that God has revealed himself to men and that those men who in faith accept this revelation thereby attain knowledge of God. Of course, not every believer is a theologian if we restrict this term to the sense it would have as derived from natural theology. The man of faith is not, as such, one who has a science of God, demonstrative knowledge of God's existence and of his attributes. Nor is the man of faith necessarily a theologian in a new sense of the term deriving from a conception of theology different from natural or philosophical theology. It is this new sense of theology that we now want to examine.

While there are many texts and passages in Thomas that might serve as our guide in this matter, we shall select the treatment to be found in the exposition of the *De trinitate* of Boethius,[22] where St. Thomas asks whether divine science is concerned with things which exist without matter and motion. This text has the advantage of building on matters we have lately been looking at.

Every science, Thomas begins, studies a subject matter and considers the principles of its subject, since knowledge of the principles and causes of its subject is the perfection of science. We know that the subject matter (*genus subjectum*) of a science is to be found as the subject of the conclusion of a demonstrative syllogism, since it is precisely such syllogisms which constitute a science. In the strongest sort of demonstrative syllogism, one in which the conclusion affirms a property of the subject, the middle term is the definition of the subject. The definition of a thing expresses its formal principles. Thus, in this paradigmatic demonstrative syllogism, it is the constitutive principles of the subject which explain its possession of the property. The principles of a subject are, however, of two kinds, Thomas remarks. Some principles are in themselves complete natures or things that are nonetheless causally explanatory of other things. As example he cites the way in which heavenly bodies, things in themselves, are causal principles with respect to earthly bodies.

Principles of this kind can pertain to a science as the causes of its subject, but they can also constitute the subject of a distinct science. The second kind of principle is that we cited in referring to the strongest type of demonstrative syllogism, principles which are not in themselves complete natures or things, but are only principles of complete natures or things, for example, unity of number, point of line, matter and form of physical body. Principles of this sort are considered only in the science concerned with the things of which they are the principles as with its subject matter.

Just as for any determinate genus or subject matter there are common principles which extend to everything contained within that genus, so there are common principles which extend to every being just insofar as it is a being. These common principles of being are of two kinds. Some are *common by way of predication*, they can be said of any being whatsoever in the way in which 'form' is predicable of all forms; others are *common by way of causality*, in the way in which numerically one sun is a principle with respect to all generable things. Those principles common to all beings in the first way are said to be common by way of analogy, that is, all beings have the analogously same principles. As for the second kind of common principles of being, what is meant is this: there are certain numerically distinct things which are principles of all other things. For example, the principles of accidents are reduced to the principles of substance, and the principles of corruptible substances are reduced to incorruptible substances as to their principles, and thus by a kind of graded order all beings are reduced back to numerically distinct principles. These ultimately explanatory principles of all beings are beings in the fullest sense, and this entails, for reasons we need not here go into, that they are separate from matter and motion. Such beings, Thomas says, may be called divine because, as Aristotle said, if the divine obtains anywhere it must be in such immaterial and unchangeable things.

These divine things which are the principles of all beings and are nonetheless distinct things in themselves can be considered in two ways: first, insofar as they are the common principles of all beings, of being as being; second, insofar as they are themselves distinct things. Nonetheless, because such principles, although in themselves they are maximally intelligible, relate to our minds as does the sun to the eye of a nightbird, they cannot be known by us except insofar as we are led to knowledge of them from their effects. And this is precisely how they are treated by the philosopher, a way suggested by St. Paul's remark that the invisible things of God can be known through created effects.

Hence divine things of this sort are treated by philosophers only insofar as they are principles of all things, and therefore are treated in that science where what is common to all beings is studied, whose subject is being as being, a science philosophers call divine science. There is however another way of knowing such things, not as they are manifested through their effects, but as they have manifested themselves. This way is mentioned by the Apostle in *First Corinthians,* 2:11 ff. "What is of God no one knows save the spirit of God. We however do not accept the spirit of this world, but the spirit which is from God, in order that we might know." And, in the same place, 2:10: "God has revealed it to us through his spirit." In this way divine things are treated as they subsist in themselves and not merely insofar as they are principles of things.[23]

Thus it is that Thomas distinguishes two kinds of divine science or theology. First, there is that divine science which considers divine things, not as the subject of the science, but as principles of the subject, and this is the theology which the philosophers pursue and which is also known as metaphysics. Second, there is a divine science which considers divine things in themselves as the subject of the science, and this is the theology which is conveyed in Holy Scripture.

We shall have to say many more things before this distinction between the two kinds of theology becomes clear, but for the moment we can appreciate that the difference stressed here is indeed striking, namely, whether the divine is the cause of the subject of the science (natural or philosophical theology) or itself the subject of the science (supernatural or scriptural theology). If the former theology is in principle accessible to any man, the latter presupposes that one accepts Scripture as conveying truths about God. But such an acceptance is what is meant by faith. Therefore, the second and new kind of theology Thomas is speaking of here is restricted to men of faith, and it will be concerned with those truths about himself that God has revealed, and which would otherwise have remained unknown.

Returning now to the question he is addressing, Thomas says that both theologies are concerned with things that exist apart or separate from matter and motion, but differently insofar as there are two ways of understanding the phrase "separate from matter and motion." In a first sense, it might be of the very nature or definition of a thing that is said to be separate that it can in no way exist in matter and motion, things like God and the angels. In another sense, a thing may be such that it is not of its nature or definition that it be in matter and motion, but it *can* be apart from matter and motion although sometimes it is found in matter and motion; things like being and substance and potency and act are separate from matter and motion because they do not need to exist in matter in motion, unlike mathematicals whose dependence on matter is such that, although they can be considered or understood without sensible matter, they do not exist apart from sensible matter. Philosophical theology is concerned with things separate from matter and motion in this second sense, whereas the theology conveyed by Holy Scripture is concerned with things separate from matter and motion in the first sense.

We see that the distinction between the two kinds of theology depends upon the givenness of faith; without faith, without the acceptance as true of what God has revealed, there would not be a theology distinct from natural or philosophical theology. Indeed Thomas distinguishes two kinds of truth about God. "Some things which are true of God exceed in every way the capacity of human reason to understand, for example, that God is three and one. Some truths are such that they can be attained by natural reason, such as, that God exists, that He is one, and the like, which even philosophers have demonstratively proved of God, led by the light of natural reason."[24] If the Trinity of Persons in God exceeds the capacity of human reason, it is clear that it cannot be understood, and, if not understood, it is difficult to see in what sense it can be the concern of a science or theology. The acceptance as true of what is not understood is a description of faith, and this is clearly a different mental stance than knowledge. The twofold distinction of truths about God would thus seem to be a distinction between what is known about God and what is believed about God. On several occasions, St. Thomas speaks of those truths about God which are accessible to unaided natural reason as preambles of faith (*praeambula fidei*). A consideration of the force and meaning of this phrase will cast further light on the two theologies.

V Faith and Theology

One of the puzzling things about Thomas's insistence that some truths about God can be known by unaided human reason, that is, independently of faith, is that the truths he has in mind are surely among those that believers believe. Nonetheless, the distinction he is making is not meant to be merely historical, as if at one time such truths as that there is a God and only one God were arrived at by means of proofs whereas now proofs have given way to faith. He himself spends quite a bit of time devising and defending proofs of God's existence. It is inevitable that we should wonder about the status of such proofs for the believer. Thomas believed from his mother's knee the truth of the proposition "There is a God." This truth is an object of his faith. Yet he is saying that this same truth is, for philosophers, an object of knowledge. Is he himself to be numbered among those philosophers? If so, what happens to the distinction between believed and known truths? If not, what is the point of his patient elaboration of proofs? It seems inescapable to conclude that "There is a God" is at once an object of knowing and of believing, at least in the sense that some men know it and others believe it. St. Thomas insists that the same truth cannot be known and believed by the same person at the same time. Does this mean that once the believer succeeds in fashioning a sound proof, he ceases to be a believer? Does this mean that believed truths can be changed into known truths and is that perhaps the function of the new kind of the-ologian Thomas would distinguish from the philosophical theo-

logian? These and other difficult questions seem to lurk behind
the phrase *praeambula fidei.*

A. Some Mental Acts

To follow Thomas here we must first get clear on the difference between knowing and believing, a difference Thomas de-
velops with reference to yet other mental acts or mental states.[25]
One knows or believes that something or other is true. Thus
we can express the objects of these mental acts by the variable
for a proposition, p. What we want to know, accordingly, is
Thomas's understanding of the difference between "knowing
that p" and "believing that p." In discussing this difference,
Thomas will add to the mix such mental acts as "thinking
(opining) that p" and "doubting that p."

(1)   When I know that p, p is true and $-p$ is false.

Values for p are such that they are either true or false.
Knowledge is had when there is a determination of the truth
of p. St. Thomas's way of expressing himself derives from the
following elementary consideration. If p is either true or false,
then if p is true, $-p$ is false, and if $-p$ is true, p is false. Thus
Thomas will say that, in knowing, the mind assents determinately
to one side of a contradiction. To know that p is to know that
p is true and that $-p$ is false.

We may recall here the distinction Thomas draws between
knowing as *intelligere* (*intellectus*) and knowing as *scire*
(*scientia*). In a narrow and proper sense of knowing, our
determination of the truth of p is inferred from the truth of
other propositions; to know something in this sense is mediated
cognition. For Thomas, as we have seen, *scire* and *scientia* are
tied to syllogism, so much so that the object of science or knowledge is the conclusion of a demonstrative syllogism known to
be true because it validly follows from true premises. Not every
proposition to which the mind gives determinate assent is
mediate, however. Thomas also allows for immediate or self-
evident truths, that is, propositions which are such that the
connection between predicate and subject is not grasped through
a middle term but is grasped as soon as one knows the meanings
of the constitutive terms. Needless to say, for Thomas, knowing

what the terms mean is not simply a matter of knowing how we use words. When I know the whole is greater than its part, this is not simply to know a truth about 'whole' and 'part,' but about wholes and parts. But that is a long story.

(2) When I think (opine) that p, $-p$ may be true.

Opinion embraces a proposition whose contradictory might turn out to be true. Needless to say, there are some values of p such that p and $-p$ can be simultaneously true. Some men have beards and some men do not have beards. In such a case, p and $-p$ are not contradictories. We have contradictories only when, if p is true, $-p$ is false, and if $-p$ is true, p is false. When we think or opine that p, we do not with confidence or certainty reject $-p$ as false. In the case of knowledge, whether it bears on self-evident truths or, in the proper sense of the term, on mediated or inferred truths, the contradictory is determinately excluded. The object of opinion may also be arrived at as a conclusion from premises, but the premises do not express evidence that is conclusive for the truth of p. No doubt there are degrees of opinion. Perhaps that is why doubt can be associated with opinion.

(3) When I doubt that p, I think or opine that $-p$.

To think or opine that $-p$ is not to be completely sure of $-p$, and thus to fear that p may be true. This is not to say that in thinking that $-p$, I equally think that p. If the evidence indicates the truth of $-p$, I will doubt that p. To hold that p or $-p$ is not to have an opinion. A jury that reported that the accused is either innocent or guilty as charged has not delivered a verdict.

Perhaps this can suffice as a sketch of "knowing that p" and "thinking that p" and "doubting that p." For our purposes, knowing and opining or thinking are the most important mental states, since it is with reference to them that Thomas will express what he means by "believing that p." It may be well to say here once and for all that Thomas, like ourselves, often uses "thinking" or "opining" to express what has here been defined as "knowing." So too he will often use "knowing" and "believing" interchangeably, and the same can be said of "believing" and "thinking." What we have just witnessed is his assigning of definite meanings for these terms for a specific purpose. In doing this, Thomas appeals to the way we talk, being guided by ordinary Latin just as we should be by ordinary English, but he is not engaged in an effort to say what these terms ordinarily or always mean in every usage. The fact that "think" and "know" and "believe" can be interchangeable in some contexts is, while true, not helpful when our purpose is to assign meanings to these terms which will distinguish different mental acts or states. It is the mental acts which differ, even though we sometimes speak of them one way and sometimes in another. Once the difference between the mental acts is clear, "know" and "think" and "believe" can be given more or less technical meanings that will cause the remarks in which they occur to diverge slightly from ordinary talk.

Given his quasi-technical accounts of "knowing that p" and "thinking that p," St. Thomas adds his account of "believing that p."

> (4)   We believe that p is true and that $-p$ is false on the basis of authority.

Armed with his definitions, Thomas will argue for the following theses:

> (5)   It is impossible for a person simultaneously to know that p and to believe that p.
>
> (6)   It is impossible for a person simultaneously to think that p and to believe that p.

If "believing that p" differs from both "knowing that p" and "thinking that p," belief nonetheless bears similarities to both knowledge and opinion. In common with "knowing that p," "believing that p" totally excludes the possibility that $-p$ might be true. To believe that p is true is to have no doubt that $-p$ is false. In common with "thinking that p," "believing that p" is not grounded on conclusive evidence of the truth of p. For purposes of completeness, we can add that "believing that p" is unlike the "knowing that p" that occurs when the value of p is a self-evident truth.

If like "knowing that p," "believing that p" entails the falsity of $-p$, this is not because the believed p follows validly from true premises, nor is it because, as with "thinking that p," the preponderance of the evidence indicates the truth of p. I may think that Notre Dame will defeat Alabama and I may think that bald-headed males are more amorous than their hirsute confreres. In both cases, I may marshal evidence to support my claim, even as I agree that one who maintains the contrary is not willfully opaque, ignorant, obtuse, and so on. In the case of belief in the Trinity or Incarnation, on the other hand, it makes little sense to say that the evidence seems to indicate their truth. One's assent to the truth of p and his rejection of $-p$ as false is explained, in the case of belief, not by conclusive evidence, but by reliance on authority.

B. Two Kinds of Belief

It will be seen that, in this discussion, St. Thomas is concerned to clarify the nature of religious belief. Nonetheless, we can get some help toward understanding the contrasts he is drawing by appealing to instances of belief that involve one man's trusting in another. Let us say that, in conversation with you, I assert that p, and you ask me why I say that. I answer that my Uncle Seymour told me that p. My assertion that p reposes on the fact that I trust my Uncle Seymour. I did not mention him when I asserted that p, in the scenario I have in mind, but, if pressed, I would admit to this avuncular source of my confidence. Let us assign a value to p. Let us imagine that what I said was, "People who lay their ungloved hands on hot stoves get burned." You asked why I say this and I bring in Uncle Seymour. I could of course be the empirical type and arrange for a hot stove to lay my ungloved hand on. More cautiously, I could secrete myself in a broom closet and observe the reactions of others when they laid their ungloved hands on the hot stove. Then when you ask me why I say that p, I need no longer bring in Uncle Seymour as the explanation of my assertion.

This situation can be generalized. The student of science or the specialist in a given area of science may assert that p, where the value of p is some scientific result, and yet reply, when pressed, that he asserts that p because Professor Seymour said so or because he has just read an article in the *Alaskan Journal of Tropical Studies*. In such cases, believing that p is of course in principle replaceable by knowing that p. Trust or faith in such a case, the acceptance of p as true on the basis of authority, need not be a terminal mental state but only a stage on the way to knowledge. *Oportet addiscentem credere*, Aristotle said: the student must trust or believe, but not because that is his goal. His goal is knowledge.[26]

In the case of religious belief, believing that p is the acceptance of the truth of p (and the falsity of $-p$) on the authority of another and is, moreover, a mental state or attitude toward p that cannot, at least in this life, be replaced by knowing that p. When the believer asserts that there is a Trinity of Persons in God or that Christ is both God and man, the basis of his conviction is the authority of God. As St. Thomas puts it, the formality under which assent is given to one side of a contradiction in the act of faith is *Deus revelans*: God revealing.[27]

The distinction between knowledge and opinion, on the one hand, and faith, on the other, seems to come down to a distinction between evidence and motive. When I assert a self-evident truth, the evidence is intrinsic to the judgment made. When I assert a mediated truth, as I do in both knowledge and opinion, the grounds, or evidence, for what I assert is found elsewhere than in the proposition I assert. The *elsewhere*, of course, refers to the premises from which the proposition is derived as a conclusion. If the evidence, whether conclusive or probable, of the conclusion is said to be extrinsic to it, it is not extrinsic in the same way or to the same degree that the motive for assent to a believed truth is. My knowledge that the internal angles of a plane triangle add up to 180° may be necessarily derived from other truths, and my opinion that life exists only on earth may be grounded in a great deal of information, but in both cases there is a connection between the proposition known or opined and the propositions which express the evidence from which it is concluded. One need only think of the relation between the terms of a syllogism. In the case of belief, the motivation for assent, namely, the trustworthiness of the authority, is quite extrinsic to the content of the proposition believed. I may have good grounds for trusting Uncle Seymour, but those grounds are not evidence for the truth of the claim I now take his word for.

It has been suggested earlier that there are two kinds of belief, the ordinary kind in which we take another's word that something is the case, and the extraordinary kind where our authority is God revealing. Let us use subscripts to distinguish them.

(4a) When I believe$_1$ that p, I accept p as true on someone's say-so, but I can in principle establish the truth or probability of p and thus dispense with the appeal to someone's say-so.

(4b) When I believe$_2$ that p, I accept p as true on God's say-so or authority, and I cannot, in this life, replace my dependence on his authority with knowledge that p is true.

Values of p as the object of believing$_2$ would be such truths as "There are three persons in one divine nature" and "Christ has both a human and divine nature." In believing$_1$, so long as my mental state is one of belief, I have a motive for assenting to or accepting the proposition as true, but I have no evidence for it. The same is true of believing$_2$, with the addendum that my condition is not even in principle corrigible or alterable in this life.

In the case of believing$_1$, when attention is shifted from the content of the proposition believed to be true to our motive for thinking so, we can of course inquire into our justification for thinking that so-and-so is trustworthy. Thus, it might be said that in trusting Uncle Seymour on the truth of p, we are believing both p and Uncle Seymour. St. Thomas will say that we believe someone and something.[28] This does not preclude our having reasons for trusting our source. In the case of believing$_1$, that justification may be found in the fact that on many past occasions Uncle Seymour has told me things that I took to be true on his say-so and subsequently found to be true on the basis of evidence. The scientist might give as justification for his taking as true what he reads in a learned journal the fact that sometimes in the past he has established the truth of its reports. Believing$_1$, taking another's word for the truth of something, can thus be seen to be an expedient, a *pis aller*, a corrigible condition, since in any given instance of it p can in principle be known, established on the basis of evidence.

Of course it would be practically impossible to verify every claim accepted on the word of others in the scientific community, say, but this is a practical and not a theoretical constraint.

The veracity or trustworthiness of the authority on whom we rely for our conviction of the truth of p when we believe$_2$ that p is a different matter. It would not do to suggest that since divine revelation has proved its veracity in the case of the Trinity, I am justified in relying on it in the case of the Incarnation, or vice versa. All instances of believing$_2$ would seem to be on the same footing. We might try to circumvent the problem in one fell swoop by saying that God is truth or that God is veracious, and that therefore it makes no sense to doubt what God says. Any human witness is fallible and might mislead, but God, being what and who he is, cannot deceive. Now the assertion that God can neither deceive nor be deceived occurs in the Act of Faith and this suggests that God's veracity is an object of faith, is itself within the circle of faith, and thus could not be external to it as a truth which props up or supports the truths constitutive of faith. We cannot show that faith is reasonable by invoking what is itself an object of faith. While all this is undoubtedly true, what Thomas calls the preambles of faith suggest a way in which it can be claimed that trusting God can be rationally grounded, by appeal to something independent of faith. Furthermore, signs, wonders, and miracles clearly have a preparatory role with regard to faith. We will return to Thomas's views on these matters. First we must clarify the meaning of preambles of faith.

C. Preambles of Faith

That clarification requires the distinctions we have made among knowing, opining, doubting, believing$_1$, and believing$_2$. The phrase, *praeambula fidei*, is taken to cover those truths about God which can be known by men independently of revelation. In other words, the so-called preambles of faith are possible objects of knowledge. The truths of faith are not, of course, possible objects of knowledge.

Let us recall the thesis set down earlier which we said followed from the clarifications and definitions we have been engaged in making.

(5)   It is impossible for a person simultaneously to know that p and to believe that p.

We now see that this means it is impossible for a person at one and the same time to accept something as true on evidence and not to accept it as true on evidence, or to accept something as true merely on another's say-so and not to accept something as true merely on another's say-so, at the same time and in the same respect. This thesis can be construed in a number of ways, given our distinction between two kinds of believing. (5) is true as it stands of both kinds of believing, but it has different implications insofar as it is understood of the one kind of belief or the other.

(5a)   It is impossible for the same person simultaneously to know that p and to believe₁ that p.

The point of this restatement is to bring out the fact that objects of believing₁ can also be objects of knowledge. The teacher may know an astronomical truth and the pupil believe₁ the same truth on the teacher's say-so, the two mental acts bearing on the same truth at the same time. And the same person can believe₁ that p at t_1 and know that p at t_2.

(5b)   It is impossible for any man in this life to know that p if p is an object of believing₂.

This is the strongest form of the thesis. With it before us, let us take as examples of preambles of faith that there is a God and that there is only one God. While it would be difficult to give a complete list of the preambles of faith, we will shortly state the criteria for any truth counting as such a preamble.

Preambles of faith are distinguished from truths of faith, the mysteries of faith. The former are truths about God which can be *known* by men relying on their natural powers alone. The truths of faith, on the other hand, would seem to be those truths about himself which God has revealed to men. The truths or mysteries of faith are such that, had they not been revealed by God, we would have remained unaware of them; they are accepted as true because God has revealed them and not, indeed never in this life, because we understand them and thus know them to be true.

Needless to say, the claim that truths of faith cannot be known by us means that they cannot be understood by us. We know them in the sense of knowing what has been proposed for our belief; we can know what God has revealed without knowing it in the sense of understanding it.

Relying on *Romans* 1:19–20, St. Thomas holds that men can, from the visible things of this world, come to knowledge of the invisible things of God.[29] This means that the world provides evidence for the existence of God. St. Thomas held that Aristotle had fashioned a sound argument for the existence of God, and he himself proposed a number of other arguments he clearly takes to be sound and conclusive. Now this means that "God exists" or "There is a God" can be a value of p in the schema: I know that p. But is not "God exists" or "There is a God" a value for p in the schema: I believe that p? If so, neither (5) nor (5a) would be violated, but surely it is (5b) that comes into play. Does not the believer believe that there is a God because God has revealed himself? But if he believes$_2$ that there is a God, then it cannot be known that there is a God according to (5b). This instance is fundamental, of course, but the very way in which Thomas speaks of the preambles of faith seems to threaten the notion with incoherence. The preambles of faith are those truths that God has revealed which can nonetheless be known. But if they are revealed, they must all be believed$_2$. And then (5b) gives trouble not only for one instance but for the whole set of preambles of faith. St. Thomas's position here would therefore seem to be incoherent.

To see how St. Thomas avoids contradicting himself, we must allow that the faith of the religious believer comprises both believing$_1$ and believing$_2$. That is, it would seem to be a common state of affairs for the religious believer to accept on the authority of divine revelation both truths about God which are in principle knowable and truths about God which are not knowable in this life. One brought up in the faith would believe that there is a God and that there is only one God, that he is intelligent, etc., where the *etc.* is meant to embrace any or all preambles of faith. But preambles of faith are by definition knowable in principle. Nor would the believer normally distinguish these from such other believed truths as the Trinity and Incarnation. But if God's existence can be known and if a believer comes to know it, he can no longer be said to believe this truth. The doctrine of preambles of faith thus comes down to this: among the things the religious person believes on the authority of divine revelation, there are some truths which are really objects of believing₁, although the bulk of the objects of his faith are objects of believing₂. When this is recognized, there is no inconsistency in saying that one who first believed that there is a God comes to know that there is a God. (5a) applies to this situation, whereas (5b) applies to those objects which are *de fide, mysteria,* objects of believing₂.

Because he holds that there are sound arguments for the existence of God and that we can come to know some of the attributes of God, St. Thomas holds that some of the truths about God that we have believed from our mother's knee are in principle knowable. Thus, insofar as they are objects of belief, they are in much the same class as those truths we accept on the authority of Uncle Seymour. Not every truth about God, indeed only a few, that we have believed from our mother's knee can be known in the sense of understood by us. Here faith is the only way in which they could be held to be true. Thus religious faith comprises believing₁ and believing₂, and the preambles of faith are the object of the former, while what is a mystery of faith is the object of the latter.

We need further clarifications. How can something that we believe be recognized as a preamble of faith? Why should God reveal to men things that men can know? Is it reasonable to give our assent to claims we cannot know and understand? Is the God of the philosophers the same as the God of revelation?

1. Criteria for Preambles

The following would seem to be the criteria for preambles of faith. Those truths about God which have been proposed for our belief but which can be understood, that is, known, because they can be derived from or deduced from other known truths, are preambles of faith and not properly of faith or *de fide.* Thomas's conception of human intellection leads him, as we have seen, to the view that the proper object of the human mind is the nature of physical objects. Thus, as a general rule, what can be known by us will be the natures and properties and accidents of physical objects. The scope of knowledge is broadened by the recognition that, by reflecting on it as it bears on the natures of physical objects, our intellection is not itself a physical activity. This suggests that other than physical things can be known by us to the degree that they are made manifest from our knowledge of the physical. The same is true of knowledge of God. To the degree that his existence and some of his attributes can be known from what we know of physical objects, he too comes, to that degree, within the range of human understanding. Some of the things that have been revealed by God about himself are like this. The application of the criteria is twofold, historical and speculative, though these are not fully distinct. By historical I mean this: insofar as Thomas finds that prior to or independently of revelation men have devised proofs for truths that have been revealed, he can conclude that those truths need not have been revealed. Of course, this presupposes that on analysis the proposed proofs are judged to be sound. Thus, the historical application of the criteria of preambles of faith involves the speculative task of assessing and/or formulating sound proofs for the truths about God in question. There is therefore no a priori way of telling which revealed truths are preambles of faith, though tradition and the common consent of the faithful have labelled some truths as mysteries of faith, truths like the Trinity, the Incarnation, the forgiveness of sins, and so forth. Even of the mysteries of faith, proofs have been sought, but with results that seem at least in retrospect to have been predictable. "Notice that (the truth) that God is three and one is believable alone and can in no wise be demonstratively proved, although for it some non-necessary arguments have been fashioned which are not very probable except to the believer."[30]

2. Why Reveal the Knowable?

Why has God revealed to men truths that are naturally knowable? Thomas holds that it is fitting that both preambles of faith as well as mysteries of faith have been proposed to us for belief. If preambles of faith were left to human inquiry alone, several unfortunate results would ensue. First, few men would have knowledge of God since there are many impediments to the arduous inquiry needed for such knowledge, among them the lack of natural talent, the want of the requisite leisure, and finally lassitude. Second, the few who did achieve demonstrable knowledge of God would do so only after a long period of time. This follows from the fact that metaphysics presupposes for its pursuit almost the totality of other knowledge. Thus the young, both because of their lack of the prerequisite knowledge and because they are distracted by passion and emotion, would not be among those who know there is a God. Third, even such knowledge of God as is laboriously and after much expenditure of time achieved would have the admixture of error and falsity. For all these reasons, Thomas concludes, it is both fitting and an index of the divine mercy that even knowable truths about God have been revealed so that certainty about such important matters can be had from the outset.[31]

3. Accepting What Cannot be Understood

Is it reasonable to give our assent to claims that cannot in principle be understood by us in this life? This is of course a most important question. Is believing$_2$ a rational act, an act in accord with human nature, or does it go against the human grain, denying and flouting the universally human? It is not unheard of to find religious believers who insist that the mysteries of faith are in conflict with what we know, that revealed truth overturns and upsets mere human calculation, that faith is, humanly considered, an absurdity. There is something to be said for this, if only because it echoes St. Paul's remark that our faith is a scandal and a folly to Jew and Gentile. In some sense of the term, religious faith goes against the human grain. If we insist that every truth must be intelligible to us, if we make our capacity to understand the measure of intelligibility and truth, then faith will seem a scandalous folly. It is far more characteristic of Thomas, however, to insist on the way in which faith perfects and brings to fruition our most basic natural desires. More specifically, he will argue that to believe—because God has revealed them—truths that we cannot comprehend is rational and justifiable.

Thomas discusses this question in Chapters 5 and 6 of the First Book of the *Summa contra gentiles*, but rather than recount what he says there, let us fashion an argument from the concept of preambles of faith. In the case of believing₁, as we have seen, taking something to be true on someone's say-so is replaceable by coming to know the truth in question. Prior to acquiring knowledge of the truth, one could say that his belief in it is reasonable because he could come to know it. That is, we do not take someone's word for the truth of something that we know to be false. And if we do not know it to be true when we believe it, we nonetheless believe that it is true. It is that antecedent conviction that is sustained when we do indeed come to know it. Furthermore, since it is practically impossible to convert all our beliefs into items of knowledge, we would take it to be reasonable to trust a source which has proved in some instances to be trustworthy. Even if in the rare case our Uncle Seymour should mislead us, the fact that for the most part he does not makes it reasonable to trust him even in the rare case. Very well. If now we consider that the preambles of faith are among the things that God has revealed, and if it is the case that these can be known after having been believed, then we might argue that the rest of what God has revealed, the mysteries of faith, are also intelligible in themselves, if not now to us. And of course it must be added that the acceptance of the mysteries of faith as true in this life is done with the conviction that in the next life what these propositions express will be seen to be the truth.

What such an argument amounts to is not a demonstration of the truth of the mysteries of faith; rather it hopes to show that, since some of the things that have been revealed can come to be known to be true, it is reasonable to accept the rest as true even though they are not understood and thus not yet known to be true.

4. The God of the Philosophers

Is the God of the philosophers the same as the God of faith? The most basic of the preambles of faith is surely that there is a God. Indeed, it can be said that any other truth that we believe implies this one, namely, that there is a God. That God is one nature and three persons, that Christ is both God and man, make sense only on the assumption that there is a God. This suggests a logical sense of the phrase "preambles of faith." Furthermore, as a preamble of faith, the truth that there is a God involves, for Thomas, the claim that there are sound proofs for the existence of God. It has been held that, even if it is allowed that there are sound proofs for the existence of God, the God who is thereby proved to exist is not the same as the God believers believe to exist. On this interpretation, the difficulties we saw with (5b) would not arise, since it is not what was believed that would come to be known. Let us look more closely at this, since it is a perennial source of contention.

The position we now wish to sketch would have it that the proposition "God exists" does not have the same valence when it is the conclusion of a demonstration, and thus a philosophical achievement, that it has when it is an object of faith. Pascal distinguished the God of the philosophers from the God of Abraham and Isaac, thereby suggesting that the God who is known is not the God who is believed.[32] The position may perhaps be developed in this way. It is clear from St. Thomas's presentation of the Five Ways of proving the existence of God[33] that he does not think that "God exists" would ever as such appear as the conclusion of a proof. After each proof, he observes that what has been shown to exist is what we mean by God.[34] What occurs as the subject of the proposition which is the conclusion of the proof is a determinate description of God, for example, first unmoved mover, first efficient cause, ultimate final cause, and so on. It is this plurality of descriptions which makes possible a plurality of proofs of God's existence. We can now put the Pascalian point this way: God is known to exist or is proved to exist under descriptions which differ from those self-descriptions God provides in revelation. It was Thomas's contemporary Bonaventure's contention that one can simultaneously know and believe the same truth,[35] for example, that God is one, a contention that conflicts with (5), (5a), and (5b). Bonaventure's subsequent exposition, however, makes clear that the object of simultaneous belief and knowledge is not really an identical object. If one can know and believe at the same time that God is one, this is so because Bonaventure interprets this to mean that one knows there is not a plurality of gods and believes that the unique God is a Trinity of Persons. Since "one" is taken in several senses, "there is one God" is not the same proposition as known and as believed.

We have interpreted Pascal's point about the God of the philosophers and the God of Abraham to mean that God is known under some descriptions and is believed under quite different descriptions. Bonaventure's claim that we can know and believe the same truth was seen to be a version of this. Now, while there is nothing incoherent about this position as stated, it is questionable whether its assumptions are true. If we should say, for example, that the philosopher may come to know God as first cause (and Thomists who think that Thomas granted Aristotle too much in interpreting the Greek philosopher as proving this must allow that Thomas himself fashioned such a philosophical proof), it is difficult to see how knowing God in this way differs from what believers have believed of him from their mother's knee. Do we not, in the creed, profess our belief in God as creator of heaven and earth? True, there are those who suggest that creation is a theological concept, apparently meaning by that that apart from faith one cannot grasp the total dependence of all else on God, which is the import of *creatio ex nihilo*.[36] While this contention, if true, would preserve the radical difference between knowledge and faith, the difference seems bought at too high a price. Indeed, it seems headed in the direction of saying that whatever philosophers claim to know about God is false.

In any case, Thomas's position is quite straightforward. If religious faith incorporates both believing$_1$ and believing$_2$ and it is possible that some believers who believed$_1$ that there is a God later come to know that there is a God, surely it is the same truth that was once believed and is now known. We would make a shambles of the concept of preambles of faith if we should say that the objects of believing$_1$ differ formally from what men can in principle know. For this reason, the Pascalian point, *unless it is restricted to believing$_2$*, is unacceptable. With respect to some descriptions of God, the God of the philosophers and the God of believers (as believing$_1$), is the same.

A parallel situation in Thomistic doctrine is found in the case of natural law. Many truths of practice have been revealed to men by God which in principle need not have been because they are naturally knowable by men. The precepts of the decalogue, the Ten Commandments, are natural law precepts according to St. Thomas. God told men that murder is wrong, although this is a truth that men can grasp independently of God's say-so. Such precepts have been revealed and thus can be accepted on the authority of God, but they are, so far as their content goes, knowable independently of divine revelation. God told men that murder is wrong, but it is not wrong simply because God said so, and in insisting on the principle, one is not demanding religious faith of those who have not got it. But surely all this would be nonsense if it were not the same precept that can either be accepted on authority or known to be true.[37]

The animus against the concept of preambles of faith, particularly as it is associated with traditional natural theology, arises from the apparent connotations of the term "preamble." St. Thomas seems to have accepted this term because he felt it expressed well the general maxim that grace presupposes nature, builds on it, and does not destroy it.[38] He does not, however, mean to suggest that the community of believers consists by and large of people who, having first acquired knowledge of God—that he exists, is one, and so on—come to believe$_2$ truths that he has revealed of himself. The fact is that revelation includes things knowable in principle as well as things that can never be understood in this life, and religious believers do not as a rule distinguish the one kind of truth from the other. But if the concept of preambles of faith does not entail that natural theology is chronologically prior to faith in the strong sense, it does mean that some of the truths to which we have given our religious assent are knowable *in via* and thus can be seen to be objects of believing$_1$. Our condition relative to them is not unlike the belief of the scientist that certain claims he himself has not verified are nonetheless true. As for St. Thomas, it is abundantly clear that his contention that the objects of believing$_1$ can be replaced by knowledge in no way commits him to the thesis that, in this life, the objects of believing$_2$ can be known to be true or be understood.

5. Preambles and Mysteries of Faith

Let us return to the most delicate matter of all. If some of the truths to which we have given the assent of faith can be known, what is the importance of this knowledge, when and if had, for those truths which are and remain *de fide*, of faith in the strong sense, believing₂? It will be appreciated how easily the claim that men can come to know and understand truths that they previously believed could be misunderstood if we had not distinguished believing₁ and believing₂. And yet, do we not want to say that believing₂ is in some way affected by the success of the program suggested by the concept of pre-ambles of faith? We have already indicated how it permits us to say that it is reasonable to assent to truths we do not and cannot in this life understand. Let us be clear how it is not affected. The fact that we can come to know a truth that we previously believed₁, for example that there is a God and only one God, in no way diminishes the necessity that the believer, be he wise or simple, accept as true, solely on the authority of God, the truth of the Trinity, of the Incarnation, of the Resurrection, of the Forgiveness of Sins, and so forth. The most accomplished metaphysician is in exactly the same condition as the most unsophisticated sacristan with respect to what is *de fide*. What is more, and this is of crucial importance, knowing that there is a God and only one God, knowing any and all of the preambles of faith, does not entail any of the *de fide* truths. The accomplished metaphysician we mentioned may very well be a nonbeliever, and his knowledge that there is a God does not compel him to believe₂ what God has revealed of himself. It was Kierkegaard's unfounded fear that natural theology commits one to this absurdity.[39]

6. Proofs of Faith?

But are there not proofs of what is of faith in the strong sense? Signs, wonders, and miracles will occur to us as possible antecedents to the assent of faith.[40] One who produces signs and wonders, one who works miracles, gains our attention for what he says, and his miracles may serve as motives for accepting as true the claims he makes about himself. I am proceeding on the assumption, warranted by Aquinas,[41] that while a miracle or sign is observable by both the believer₂ and the unbeliever, the two interpret differently what they see. The believer interprets them as the works of God, the unbeliever does not. The reasons are complex but may be suggested by the following: crowds saw and heard and witnessed Christ, yet not everyone believed him to be what he claimed to be. Of those who saw and heard and did not believe, we cannot say that in witnessing works they recognized as divine, they did not recognize them as divine. To see a miracle as a miracle presupposes faith and does not precede faith.[42]

We have reached a point where, thanks to the distinction between knowledge and faith, we can better understand the distinction Thomas makes between two kinds of theology, philosophical theology, on the one hand, and the theology based on Holy Scripture, on the other. The latter presupposes faith but is not identical with it. But before seeing the nature of this second kind of theology and its typical tasks, we must first devote a few pages to the examination of one of the proofs that Thomas devised to show that there is a God.

VI *Proving That God Exists*

Such a proof is something that could be and, according to Thomas, has been successfully fashioned by philosophers. The interest of the theologian, in the new and second sense proposed by Thomas, in such proofs is clear from the import of the concept of preambles of faith. Such a proof, if sound, will exhibit to the believer that some of the things God has revealed, indeed that which is implicit in everything that has been revealed, are true and this will provide him with a basis for saying that it is therefore reasonable to hold that all that God has revealed is true. Furthermore, such a proof, if sound, should be seen to be so by anyone, whether or not he is a believer. Thus, in concerning himself with proofs and generally with the preambles of faith, the theologian is seeking to establish an area of communication between believer and nonbeliever. Some believers and some nonbelievers may come to agree that an argument for the existence of God is sound. As we have seen, for the non-believer to accept such a sound proof does not compel him to become a believer. Nonetheless, to have a sound proof for the existence of God removes one impediment to faith, since a man who knows there is a God knows that there is someone who could have revealed what the believer believes God has revealed.

Proofs for the existence of God divide historically into two kinds, the a priori and the a posteriori. The chief example of the first kind is the so-called Ontological Argument fashioned by St. Anselm of Canterbury in his *Proslogion*. St. Thomas gives extremely short shrift to the Anselmian proof.[43] He himself holds that any sound proof of the existence of God will have as premises known truths about beings other than God. That is, it will be a posteriori. He himself, in the *Summa theologiae*, sketches five such proofs, the famous *quinque viae*, five ways of proving that there is a God. Of the five, he holds that the first, the one from motion, is the most manifest. Nonetheless, we shall here consider his third proof.[44]

The third way of proving the existence of God is based on the possible and the necessary.

(1) Some of the things that are, since they are generated and corrupt, can either be or not be.

(2) It is impossible that everything that is should be such that it can either be or not be.

(3) Whatever is such that it can not-be at some time is not.

(4) Thus if everything were such that it could either be or not be, at some time there was nothing.

(5) But if once there was nothing, there would be nothing now, since that which from not being comes to be requires a cause which is.

(6) Therefore if once there was nothing, nothing could have come to be, and even now there would be nothing, which is clearly false.

(7) Therefore not everything is possible and there must be something which is necessary.

(8) That which is necessary either has a cause of its necessity from elsewhere, or it does not.

(9) It is impossible that all necessary beings should have a cause of their necessity outside themselves.

(10) Therefore there must be a necessary being whose necessity is not caused by another but which is necessary of itself.

(11) Such a necessary being all call God.

It will be seen that this proof has two major stages; the first, (1)–(7), establishes a realm of necessary beings, and the second, (8)–(10), arrives at something that is necessary per se and that is taken to be descriptive of God.

In the first stage of the proof, it is the transition from (3) to (4) which seems to pose the greatest difficulty. It is easy enough to grant that a thing that has come into being did not exist at a prior time. But does it follow that if everything were of this kind, there was some prior time when nothing at all existed? If we think of human generations, for example, it is quite easy to concede that for any man there was some prior time when he did not exist, and the same would be true of his father, his grandfather, his great-grandfather, and so on and on. For anyone of them, there is a prior time when that thing did not exist. In 1920, Peter I did not exist; in 1900, Peter II did not exist; and in 1875, the eponymous Peter did not exist. Thus, a time when Peter III did not exist is a time when Peter II does exist and a time when Peter II did not exist is a time when Peter I does exist. In short, there seems no need to have one particular time at which no such thing exists simply because, for each of them, there is a prior time when it did not exist. St. Thomas would thus seem to be guilty here of a rather elementary logical error, a quantification mistake. It is not unlike the fallacy involved in moving from the truth that every road ends somewhere to the proposition that there is somewhere that each and every road ends—Rome perhaps.

Perhaps there is some way of interpreting what Thomas has said that will not involve him in so simple a mistake. Indeed, in order to make the mistake alleged, one would have to ignore just the point Thomas seems to be making. He clearly wants to say that it is incoherent to claim that everything that is has come into being since such things require a preexistent cause in order to come into being. But if the cause to which appeal is made itself came into being, then the generalized problem remains: *why should there be anything like that at all?* To say that the reason lies in the fact that there was something else like that before does not address what I am calling the generalized problem. There is a transition here from a discussion of this and that thing which has come into being to a concentration on that sort or kind of thing. And what Thomas is saying is that not everything which is could be that sort of thing. That is the point of (4). Granted the existence of such things, each of which is such that before it was it was not, there is of course no need that each member of the class not be simultaneously. But, again, if we ask why there should be things like that at all, the answer that would explain one of them by appeal to another simply begs the question.

It has been suggested that, in order to get such a series of possible beings going, one need only imagine one of them popping uncaused into existence.[45] Of course, Thomas could not accept this. Something which has come into existence must have been caused to exist; to say that its existence is uncaused is in effect to say that it is per se and that in turn is to say that it is necessary and that it could not not have existed. And this is against the hypothesis.

Is it just a matter of seeing things a certain way to suggest that it is impossible that whatever is is such that at one time it was not? Perhaps it is not a matter of two radically different ways of answering a question so much as it is a matter of honoring or not honoring the question. To return to our earlier example, of course the father is a cause of the son's coming to be, as the grandfather is a cause of the father's coming to be, but Thomas wants us to ask why there should be things of that kind at all. What the first stage of his proof seeks to establish is that in order for there to be things of this kind, things that *can* be, there must be things of another kind, things that *must* be.

The second stage of the proof may puzzle us in a quite different way. If a thing necessarily is, how can it be caused to be? One would have thought that the necessary was introduced precisely to block the need for a cause. In order to grasp the sense of this, we must notice that the examples Thomas gives of possible or contingent beings are those which are generated and which corrupt. Such beings, we have seen, are composed of matter and form. Their form determines the matter in such and such a way, but the matter remains in potency to other determinations by other forms. Thus, matter is an intrinsic and essential principle of the thing's potentiality not to be. When Thomas speaks of necessary beings, he is thinking of beings which are not composed of matter and form, but are form alone.[46] Thus there is no intrinsic essential possibility of their not being. But if there is no composition of matter and form, there is still a composition of essence and existence. Thus, such beings have no intrinsic principle of nonbeing and therefore are necessary, but they are, so to speak, extrinsically contingent, since the form that is actualized is not the actualization of that form, and there must be an extrinsic cause of that actualization. This leads Thomas to say that not every necessary being can be such that its necessity depends on another, and the procedure here is much like that followed in the first stage of the proof. The upshot is that there must be a being which necessarily and per se exists, and such a being is God.

The reader need not be told that the proof just sketched is extremely difficult to understand and consequently cannot easily be assessed pro or con. The suggestions that have been made as to how the movement of the proof should be understood are themselves open to question. Indeed, there seems to be no chance that any attempt to fashion a sound proof or to express dissatisfaction with it will soon exhaust further relevant remarks, so that such discussions must seem to the non-philosopher, and perhaps in his darker moods to the philosopher too, interminable and without issue. And that is why Thomas, even though he holds that there are sound proofs of God's existence, feels that it is fitting that God has revealed himself to man and that certainty can be had on the matter through faith while the philosophical disquisition goes on.

VII *Concluding*

When St. Thomas is said to have been a theologian, the sense of the term is taken not from metaphysics or philosophical theology but from the theology based on Holy Scripture. We have said earlier that this theology must not be equated with faith. Surely it would be absurd to suggest that each and every believer, just insofar as he is a believer, engages in the sort of intellectual reflection on faith that we find in the *Summas* and *Disputed Questions*. Theology presupposes faith and is not identical with it. And we are prepared from the foregoing to find Thomas speaking of theology on the basis of the Aristotelian conception of science. We have seen him saying that the subject of natural theology is being as being, whereas the subject of scriptural theology is God himself. Furthermore, theology as a science will be made up of arguments and proofs, it will have principles, and so on. But how can theology have principles like other sciences, if principles are assumed in the science precisely because they are self-evident? Surely there are no self-evident truths about God so far as we are concerned. Thomas holds that the principles or starting points of the science of theology are just those truths about God that God has revealed and thus they are accepted by faith. Yet even here he makes use of the Aristotelian model and notices that Aristotle allows for a science which accepts its principles from another science, such that truths assumed in the subalternated science are known or proved in the subalternating science. Thus, in natural science we may assume truths from geometry and apply them to physical bodies. In a not wholly dissimilar way, Thomas suggests, the truths that we accept on faith in this life are subalternated to the knowledge of the blessed in heaven, who do not believe but see even as they are seen.[47]

Not only is the model of science drawn from philosophical science, theology as Thomas envisages it makes use of philosophy. This can be taken to mean that the theologian brings to bear on what is believed the totality of human knowledge. He sets down three ways in which theology makes use of philosophy, and these may suffice as a statement of the tasks of theology: (1) Theology makes use of philosophy in order to prove the preambles of faith; and also (2) to cast light upon the mysteries of faith by bringing to bear on them certain similitudes, as Augustine in his *De trinitate* employs many examples from philosophy to manifest the mystery of the Trinity; (3) philosophy is useful to the theologian for the refutation of objections brought against the mysteries of faith. This employment of philosophy has its dangers, of course, since one might take a philosophical error rather than a truth and, even worse, one might proceed as if the mysteries of faith had to be entirely subjected to the canons of natural reason.[48]

Thomas would of course deny that the mysteries of faith can be inferred from what is naturally known, since this would amount to the absurd identification of faith and knowledge. But, as we have already seen, he is insistent on the fact that religious faith is a reasonable and fitting thing. It is simply false to characterize religious faith as if it were a conscious acceptance of nonsense or absurdity. God is the source of both the natural powers of reason and of revelation and it is silly to suggest that God would propose for our acceptance as true what contradicts what we naturally know to be the case. Faith is above reason, but not against reason. What the believer believes is that the object of his faith is intelligible in itself and will be seen to be so in the next world. That is why one of the major tasks of the theologian is to show that what is believed is not contradicted by what is known. He need not, because he cannot, show directly the truth of what is believed, but he can show the falsity of whatever contradicts what is believed. It is the starting point and assumption of the theologian that this can be done and, far from being a sign of his irrationality, it underscores his conviction of the reasonableness of belief. Of course, it is not necessary to show determinately the falsity of what contradicts revealed truth. It suffices to show that it is not necessarily true.

CHAPTER 6

Envoi

IT is a short distance, geographically, from Rocca Secca, where Thomas Aquinas was born, to Fossanova, where he died, but it took Thomas a lifetime to get from the one point to the other. Today the traveller can climb a higher hill above the present town of Rocca Secca and, standing among the ruins of the castle, look out over the valley Thomas would have seen as a child when, allegedly, he first asked, "What is God?" The same traveller can be shown, at Fossanova, in the former Cistercian monastery, a room on the second floor where Thomas died, convinced that all he had written of God was as straw. That conviction was the product of a mystical experience, and the traveller, unblessed by that, can only muse at the vast distance—philosophically, theologically, spiritually—Thomas travelled from childhood to the age of forty-nine when he died. What he had written then started on a journey which has not ended yet.

This book has been a journey too. Its author, looking back over it, dismayed at how little he has managed to say, is Thomist enough to think that it is straw. How can his reader discover here the Thomas who wrote the magnificent office of the feast of Corpus Christi whose hymns are still heard in our churches? How can his reader derive from these poor pages any sense of the loving meditation that went into Thomas's commentaries on Scripture? And why did the author not insist on the scholarly achievement of the *Catena aurea*, a golden chain indeed of Patristic and later expositions of the Gospels? It is easy to be impressed by the logical elegance of selected arguments of Thomas. Few can fail to be impressed by the lucidity of his analysis of particular points. But if some of the parts are here, where is the whole? Thomas is that exceedingly rare person who combines holiness, a spiritual life that rivals those of the greatest mystics, with the care and precision and

170

boundless patience of the intellectual. There are many holy people who look with disdain on arguments; there are many proficient in argument for whom holiness is a closed book. It is important, in reading Thomas, to remember that he often paused to pray when he wrote, that the writing itself was a prayer. He regarded mind as the distinctive mark of the creature man is, and it was his creaturely duty to use his mind as well as he could. But as a believer, he knew the limitations of mind. He knew that love can go a long way on the basis of a minimum of understanding. Our destiny is the perfection of knowledge, a beatifying vision of God, but that is a knowledge that will be animated by love.

It is safe to predict that Thomas's role as intellectual mentor will only increase. His status among Roman Catholics is, or at least should be, secure. Thomas has been canonized by the Church; he has been named *Doctor Communis* whose teaching the Church has made her own. He was on his way to a Church council when he died. In a way, he has attended all those that have been held since. For a Catholic not to know Thomas is to be cut off from an essential portion of his patrimony. For others, Thomas's importance for such a large segment of humanity lends him a prima facie wider cultural interest. From the *Divina Commedia* onward, Thomas speaks indirectly through vast numbers of artistic achievements, and it would be a cultural impoverishment not to know directly the thought of a man who has seemed paradigmatic to so many believers. And if Thomas is right in his thoughts on the distinction betweeen faith and knowledge, if his philosophical efforts were successful, and perhaps even if they were not, he has a claim on the attention of philosophers in general. Indeed, unbelieving philosophers seem intent on trying the steel of their refutations on Thomas's arguments in preference to all others, as if, should they be successful against him, they must surely be said to have carried the day.

It is not necessary, then, to share Thomas's religious faith in order to read him with profit, any more than one must share Dante's or Shakespeare's or Milton's or Donne's. There will doubtless always be many of those whom *Time* has called Peeping Thomists, thinkers who derive much of what they hold from the study of Thomas but who are either not believers or, if believers, not Catholics. Nonetheless, it is the believer and particularly the Catholic who will feel most drawn to Thomas. For them, the traditional precept will seem less a command than an invitation or opportunity. *Ite ad Thomam.* Go to Thomas. That is the message of this book.

Notes and References

Chapter One

1. See James Weisheipl, *Friar Thomas D'Aquino* (New York, 1974), pp. 3–12. For the reader of English alone, this work, along with Vernon Bourke's *Aquinas' Search for Wisdom* (Milwaukee, 1965), is essential.

2. Thomas Aquinas accepts this traditional division of the liberal arts. For his effort to synthesize the older plan of studies and the Aristotelian order of learning philosophy, see the exposition of Boethius's *De trinitate,* q. 5, a. 1, ad 3m.

3. See Weisheipl, pp. 17–18.

4. *Ibid.,* pp. 20–24.

5. Weisheipl's somewhat "demythologized" account may be found on p. 35 of his book. See also Bourke, pp. 33–42.

6. Weisheipl provides an excellent sketch of Albert on pp. 39–45.

7. Cf. my *Philosophy From Augustine to Ockham,* Vol. 2 of *A History of Western Philosophy* (Notre Dame, 1970), pp. 215–219; Weisheipl, *op. cit.,* p. 53 ff.

8. For a good brief treatment of Aristotle's entry into Europe, see F. Van Steenberghen, *Aristotle in the West* (Louvain, 1955).

9. A dramatic account of this detective work is to be found in H. D. Saffrey, *Sancti Thomae de Aquino Super Librum de Causis Expositio* (Fribourg, 1954), p. xv ff.

10. Weisheipl, p. 151, has some cautionary remarks on the "commissioning" of William by Thomas.

11. In *La philosophie au XIIIe Siècle* (Louvain, 1966), pp. 357–412.

12. Bourke, pp. 141–158; Weisheipl, pp. 241–292.

13. Cf. A. Dondaine, *Sécretaires de saint Thomas* (Rome, 1956).

14. Josef Pieper's *The Silence of St. Thomas* (New York, 1957) is an extended reflection on the way in which Thomas's writing and teaching ended.

15. *Summa theologiae,* IIaIIae, q. 175.

16. 2 Cor. 12:2.

Chapter Two

1. See F. Van Steenberghen, *Aristotle in the West*. (Louvain, 1955).

2. See above, Ch. 1, n. 10.

3. *Physics* 8.1.

4. F. E. Peters, *Aristotle and the Arabs* (New York, 1968).

5. *Metaphysics* 12.9.

6. For a discussion of this point, see Ralph McInerny, "Ontology and Theology in Aristotle's Metaphysics," in *Mélanges à la mémoire de Charles de Koninck*, (Quebec, 1968), pp. 233–240.

7. Van Steenberghen, *La philosophie au XIIIe Siècle* (Louvain, 1966), pp. 80–99.

8. I have used the text of the *De aeternitate mundi contra murmurantes* to be found in S. *Thomae Aquinatis Opuscula Philosophica*, ed. Spiazzi (Turin, 1954), pp. 105–108.

9. Later, in Chapter 3, we will discuss the real distinction between essence and existence in all creatures.

10. *Summa theologiae*, Ia, q. 46, a. 1.

11. *Ibid.*, Ia, q. 10.

12. *In Octo Libros Physicorum Aristotelis Expositio*, ed. (Rome, 1954): *In I Physic.*, lect. 12–13.

13. In *Opuscula philosophica*, ed. cit., p. 119 ff.

14. In commenting on Aristotle's *Metaphysics* 5.4 (*lectio* 5), Thomas discusses the many meanings of "nature."

15. On "universe," see *Summa theologiae*, Ia, q. 103, a. 3; on "cosmos" or "world," see Proemium of Thomas's commentary on Aristotle's *On Heaven and Earth*.

16. *Physics* 1.7; St. Thomas, *In I Physic.*, lect. 12, n. 5.

17. *Ibid.*, 191a9–10; *In I Physic.*, lect. 13, n. 9.

18. *On the Soul* 2.1, 412a27–8; Thomas, *In II de Anima*, lect. 2; *Summa theologiae*, Ia, q. 75, a. 1.

19. See Ralph McInerny, "Le terme 'âme', est-il univoque ou equivoque?", *Révue philosophique de Louvain*, 58 (1960), 481–504; English version in my *Studies in Analogy* (The Hague, 1968).

20. I use the text as edited by Leo Keeler, *Sancti Thomae Aquinatis Tractatus de Unitate Intellectus Contra Averroistas* (Rome, 1946).

21. *Quaestiones Disputatae*, ed. Spiazzi et al. (Turin, 1949), Vol. 1.

22. *Q. D. de Veritate* (On Truth), q. 2, a. 2.

23. This raises the "problem of universals." See below, Chapter 4.

24. See F. C. Copelston, *A History of Medieval Philosophy* (New York, 1972), pp. 199–212.

25. *In III de anima*, lect. 10.

26. *Summa theologiae*, Ia. q. 77 and q. 85, a. 1.

27. *IV Contra gentiles*, Ch. 80.

28. *In I Ethic.* (*Nicomachean Ethics*), lect. 17, n. 212.

29. *Summa theologiae*, IaIIae, prologue.

30. *Ibid.*, Ia, qq. 75–102.

31. *Ibid.*, Ia, q. 64, a. 2.

32. *On Truth*, q. 24, art. 2.

33. Commentary on Bk. 2, *lectio* 3, n. 257.

34. *In I De coelo et mundo*, lect. 26, n. 6.

35. *Summa theologiae*, Ia, q. 83, a. 1; *On Truth*, q. 24, art. 1.

36. *On Truth*, q. 2, art. 2.

37. Commentary on *On the Soul*, Bk. 2, *lectio* 5, nn. 295–298.

38. *Summa theologiae*, Ia, q. 83; *On Truth*, q. 24.

39. *Quaestio disputata de Malo*, q. 6, a. 1.

40. *Summa theologiae*, Ia, q. 83, a. 1.

41. *Ibid.*, IaIIae, q. 13, a. 6.

42. *Ibid.*, IaIIae, q. 1, a. 1.

43. ". . . actions of this kind are not properly human, because they do not proceed from the deliberation of reason, which is the proper principle of human acts." *Summa theologiae*, IaIIae, q. 1, a. 6.

44. *Ibid.*, IaIIae, q. 1, a. 5.

45. "It is necessary that whatever a man desires he desires for the sake of the ultimate end, which is clear from these two arguments. First, because whatever a man desires, he desires under the formality of good. And what is not desired as the perfect good, that is, as the ultimate end, must be desired as tending to the ultimate end." *Summa theologiae*, IaIIae, q. 1, a. 6.

46. *Nicomachean Ethics* 1.7.

47. *Summa theologiae*, IaIIae, q. 3, a. 5.

48. *Ibid.*, IaIIae, q. 3, a. 8.

49. *Ibid.*, IaIIae, q. 13, a. 6.

50. *Ibid.*, Ia, q. 14, a. 16.

51. Exposition of the *De trinitate* of Boethius, q. 5, a. 1.

52. *Summa theologiae*, Ia, q. 14, a. 16.

53. "Knowledge is said to be practical because of its being ordered to some work (*opus*), which occurs in two ways. Sometimes actually (*in actu*), namely when it is actually involved in the production of a work, as when the artisan proposes to impose a preconceived form on matter. . . . Sometimes however knowledge is indeed such that it can be ordered to act but is not actually so ordered, as when the artisan thinks of a possible artifact and knows it as the term of various steps (*per modum operandi*), but does not intend to perform

those steps; this is practical knowing *habitu vel virtute,* certainly, but not in act." *On Truth,* q. 3, a. 3.

54. *Summa theologiae,* IaIIae, q. 94, a. 4.

55. *Ibid.,* IaIIae, q. 93.

56. *Ibid.,* IaIIae, q. 90, a. 4.

57. On this point, see Ralph McInerny, "The Meaning of *Naturalis* in Aquinas's Theory of Natural Law," in *La Filosofia della Natura nel Medioevo,* ed. Vita e Pensiero (Milan, 1966), pp. 560–565.

58. "It should be said that law is a kind of dictate of practical reason. The process of practical reason is similar to that of theoretical reason since in both there is a movement from principles to conclusions. . . . Given this, we hold that just as from undemonstrable principles naturally known speculative reason derives the conclusions of the different sciences, knowledge of which is not naturally given us but is acquired by the application of reason, so too from the precepts of natural law, as from common and indemonstrable principles, the human reason proceeds to more particular judgments." *Summa theologiae,* IaIIae, q. 91, a. 3.

59. *Ibid.,* IaIIae, q. 94, a. 2.

60. There is a vast literature devoted to natural law. One way into it is via R. A. Armstrong's *Primary and Secondary Precepts in Thomistic Natural Law Teaching* (The Hague, 1966), which has a good bibliography. See too E. B. F. Midgley, *The Natural Law Tradition and the Theory of International Relations* (New York, 1975).

61. See Armstrong, Ch. 6.

62. *Summa theologie,* IaIIae, q. 95, a. 2.

63. *Ibid.,* IaIIae, q. 94, a. 4.

64. *On the Virtues in General,* trans. Reid (Providence, 1951), a. 6, ad lm.

65. *Summa theologiae,* IaIIae, q. 57, a. 5, ad 3m.

66. *Ibid.,* IaIIae, q. 90, a. 1, ad 2m.

67. *Ibid.,* IaIIae, q. 76, a. 1.

68. On this problem, see *Weakness of Will,* ed. G. W. Mortimore (New York, 1970).

69. Ralph McInerny, "Prudence and Conscience," *The Thomist,* 38, No. 2 (1974), 291–305.

70. *Summa theologiae,* IaIIae, q. 63, a. 3.

71. *On Charity,* trans. Kendzierski (Milwaukee, 1960), a. 3.

Chapter Three

1. See Boethius, *In librum de interpretatione edito secunda,* Migne, *Patrologia Latina,* Vol. 64, col. 433C. Hereafter cited as *PL.*

2. See Pierre Courcelle, *Late Latin Writers and Their Greek Sources* (Cambridge, Mass., 1969), Ch. 6.

3. See Ralph McInerny, *Philosophy from St. Augustine to Ockham* (Notre Dame, 1970), pp. 157–186.

4. *De trinitate*, Ch. 2. The Latin text with an English translation can be found in *Boethius: Theological Tractates and The Consolation of Philosophy*, ed. H. F. Stewart and E. K. Rand (New York, 1918), pp. 2–31.

5. On this, see Migne, *PL* 64, 10–11.

6. *On Truth*, q. 1, a. 12.

7. Exposition of Boethius's *De trinitate*, q. 5, a. 1.

8. *Summa theologiae*, Ia, q. 2, a. 2.

9. Exposition of *De trinitate*, q. 5, a. 1. I have added numbers and underlining.

10. On all this, see *Summa theologiae*, Ia, q. 85, a. 3.

11. See, for instance, L. B. Geiger, "Abstraction et séparation d'après Saint Thomas in de Trinitate, q. 5, a. 3," *Revue des Sciences Philosophiques et Théologiques*, 31 (1947), pp. 3–40.

12. *Summa theologiae*, IaIIae, q. 82, a. 2, ad 3m.

13. *Ibid.*, IaIIae, q. 3, a. 6; Ia, q. 1, a. 7.

14. The procedure within a science is from the more to the less common, but the latter are not deduced from the former. Thomas distinguishes the *Ordo determinandi* (from more to less universal) from the *Ordo demonstrandi*. See *In I Physic.*, lectio 1.

15. Exposition of Boethius's *De trinitate*, q. 5, a. 3. I have divided and numbered the text.

16. *Ibid.*

17. *Ibid.* "That form whose definition does not include matter can be abstracted from matter but the mind cannot abstract from matter a form the understanding of which depends on matter. Hence, since all accidents relate to substance as form to matter, and the definition of any accident depends on substance, it is impossible for such forms to be abstracted from substance. But accidents inhere in substance in an ordered way; first quantity, then quality, then passion and motion inhere in it. Hence quantity can be understood in the matter, substance, without sensible qualities being understood, qualities from which substance is called sensible matter; so, considering its formal definition, quantity does not depend on sensible matter, but only on intelligible matter (that is, on substance)."

18. *Ibid.* Cf. *Summa theologiae*, Ia, q. 85, a. 1.

19. Exposition of Boethius's *De trinitate*, q. 5, a. 3.

20. *Ibid.*, q. 5, a. 2.

21. For instance, in Ralph McInerny, "Saint Thomas Aquinas and Boethius," *Rivista di Filosofia Neo-Scolastica*, 66 (1974), 219–245.

22. Exposition of Boethius's *De hebdomadibus*, lectio 2.

23. See n. 21, above.

24. See exposition of Boethius's *De hebdomadibus*, lectio 2, n. 32.

25. *Ibid.*, " . . . just as to be and that which is differ *secundum intentiones* in simple things, so in composed things they differ *realiter.*"

26. *Ibid.*, n. 35.

27. *On Being and Essence*, Ch. 5, n. 3.

28. For Thomas, "necessary" modifies existence and not merely judgments or propositions.

29. For instance, Etienne Gilson, *Being and Some Philosophers* (Toronto, 1952).

30. *Commentary on Metaphysics*, trans. Rowan (Chicago, 1964) nn. 46, 181, 593, 690, 748, 2517.

31. Bks. 4 and 5.

32. *Summa theologiae*, Ia, q. 25, a. 3.

33. *Ibid.*

34. Charles de Koninck, "Le problème de l'indetérminisime," *L'Académie Canadienne Saint-Thomas d'Aquin* (Quebec, Canada, 1937), pp. 65–159.

35. *Summa theologiae*, Ia, q. 14, a. 9.

36. *Ibid.*, q. 14, a. 13. This definition of eternity comes from Boethius, *The Consolation of Philosophy*, ed. H. F. Stewart and E. K. Rand, New York, 1928, Bk. 5, prose 6.

37. *Summa theologiae*, Ia, q. 14, a. 13, ad 3m. On this question see A. N. Prior, "The Formalities of Omniscience," *Papers on Time and Tense* (Oxford, 1968), pp. 26–44.

38. *Summa theologiae*, Ia, q. 14, a. 13, ad 3m.

39. Commentary on Aristotle's *On Interpretation*, lectio 14.

Chapter Four

1. See, for instance, Cornelio Fabro, *La nozione metafisica di partecipazione*, 3rd ed. (Rome, 1963); and *Partecipazione e causalità* (Rome, 1960); L. B. Geiger *La participation dans la philosophie de saint Thomas d'Aquin* (Paris, 1942); R. J. Henle, *St. Thomas and Platonism* (The Hague, 1956).

2. See R. Arnou, "Platonisme des Pères," *Dictionnaire de théologie catholique* (Paris, 1929) pp. 2258–2392.

3. See, for instance, Anton-Herman Chroust, *Asistotle: New*

Light on His Life and on Some of His Lost Works, 2 vols. (London and Notre Dame, 1974).

4. *Contra academicos,* III, xvii, 37.

5. Bk. 8, Ch. 6.

6. Bk. 19, Ch. 1.

7. *The City of God,* Bk. 8, Ch. 10.

8. *Contra academicos,* III, xx, 43.

9. *Ibid.,* III, xvii, 37.

10. *Eighty-Three Diverse Questions,* Question 46.

11. See J. Durantel, *Saint Thomas et le Pseudo-Denis* (Paris, 1919).

12. See n. 1, above.

13. Porphyry was the biographer and student of Plotinus, the editor of the *Enneads,* and an opponent of Christianity. See Andrew Smith, *Porphyry's Place in the Neoplatonic Tradition* (The Hague, 1974).

14. *Summa theologiae,* Ia, q. 85, a. 1.

15. *On Being and Essence,* Ch. 3. See Joseph Bobik, *Aquinas on Being and Essence* (Notre Dame, 1965).

16. *On Being and Essence,* Ch. 3.

17. *Ibid.*

18. *Summa theologiae,* Ia, q. 15, a. 1.

19. *Ibid.*

20. Bonaventure, for example. See Ralph McInerny, *Philosophy From Augustine to Ockham* (Notre Dame, 1970), p. 276 ff.; J. F. Quinn, *The Historical Constitution of St. Bonaventure's Philosophy* (Toronto, 1973).

21. *Summa theologiae,* Ia, q. 84, a. 5.

22. *Ibid.*

23. *Ibid.*

24. Question 11 of *On Truth.*

25. In the edition of H. D. Saffrey, *Sancti Thomae de Aquino Super Librum De Causis Expositio* (Fribourg, 1954), see p. 38, line 14; pp. 67–68; p. 83, line 12; p. 104, lines 1–3.

26. Ch. 4.

27. Ch. 11.

28. *In librum beati Dionysii De divinis nominibus,* proemium.

29. *Summa theologiae,* Ia, q. 13, a. 1, ad 2m.

30. *Summa contra gentiles,* I, 30.

31. *Summa theologiae,* Ia, q. 20, a. 1, ad 2m.

32. *Ibid.,* Ia, q. 3.

33. *Ibid.,* Ia, q. 13, a. 4.

34. *In librum beati Dionysii De divinis nominibus,* Ch. 5.

35. Commentary on Aristotle's *Metaphysics*, Bk. 1, lectio 10, n. 158.
36. *Summa theologiae*, Ia, q. 4, a. 2, ad 3m.
37. Exposition of Boethius's *De hebdomadibus*, lectio 2.
38. *Summa theologiae*, Ia, q. 13, a. 11.
39. See Saffrey, *ed. cit.* (n. 25, above), p. 47.
40. *Summa theologiae*, Ia, q. 13, a. 12.
41. *On Being and Essence*, Ch. 5.

Chapter Five

1. See, on this issue, Werner Jaeger, *Aristotle: Fundamentals of the History of His Development* (New York, 1934); A. H. Chroust, *Aristotle* (London and Notre Dame, 1973); Ralph McInerny, "Ontology and Theology in Aristotle's Metaphysics," *Melanges à la mémoire de Charles de Koninck* (Quebec, 1968).
2. See Jaeger, *op. cit.*
3. Aristotle *Metaphysics* 4.1 and 4.2.
4. *Ibid.*, 6.1, 1026a27–33.
5. Thomas Aquinas, *In Metaphysicorum libros*, Proemium.
6. *Ibid.* The reader will be reminded of what Thomas said in commenting on Boethius's *De trinitate*, q. 5, a. 1.
7. In *Metaphysicorum libros*, Proemium. Jaeger seems never to have asked himself whether he himself was asking about two possible subjects of a science, understanding the phrase *ex Aristotele*.
8. *Ibid.*
9. In Aristotle *Nicomachean Ethics* 1.6.
10. See the proemia Thomas wrote to his commentaries on Aristotle's *On Interpretation* and *Posterior Analytics*.
11. Cf. Aristotle *Categories*, Ch. 1 and *Nicomachean Ethics* 1.6.
12. *Summa theologiae*, Ia, q. 13, a. 5.
13. *Ibid.*, Ia, q. 16, a. 6. See Ralph McInerny, *The Logic of Analogy* (The Hague, 1961).
14. *Summa theologiae*, Ia, q. 13, a. 1.
15. *In I Sent.*, d. 22, q. 1, a. 3, ad 2m: " . . . the equivocal, analogous and univocal are differently divided. For the equivocal is divided according to things signified (*res significatas*), the univocal according to (specific) differences, and the analogous according to diverse modes."
16. *Summa contra gentiles*, I, 34.
17. *Summa theologiae*, Ia, q. 16, a. 6.
18. That is, we are still confronted with the problem that "being is said in many ways."

19. See *Categories*, Ch. 5, and Thomas's commentary on the *Metaphysics*, Bk. 5, lectio 9.

20. *Summa theologiae*, Ia, q. 44, a. 1.

21. Commentary on *Metaphysics*, Bk. 4, lectio 1.

22. In q. 5, a. 4.

23. *Ibid.*

24. *Summa contra gentiles*, I, 3.

25. In *On Truth*, q. 14, articles 1 and 2. For another version of this, see Ralph McInerny, "The Contemporary Significance of St. Bonaventure and St. Thomas," *The Southwestern Journal of Philosophy*, 5, No. 2 (1974), 11–26.

26. *Summa theologiae*, IaIIae, q. 2, a. 3.

27. *Ibid.*, Ia, q. 1, a. 3.

28. *Ibid.*, IaIIae, q. 2, a. 2.

29. See Thomas's commentary on Paul's *Epistle to the Romans*, Ch. 1, lectio 6.

30. Exposition of Boethius's *De trinitate*, q. 1, a. 4.

31. *Summa contra gentiles*, I, 4.

32. See Romano Guardini, *Pascal For Our Times* (New York, 1966); and J. H. Broome, *Pascal* (New York, 1966).

33. *Summa theologiae*, Ia, q. 2, a. 3.

34. *Ibid.* E.g., "Therefore it is necessary that we arrive at some first mover itself unmoved by anything else, and this all understand to be God."

35. See Ralph McInerny, *Philosophy from Augustine to Ockham*, pp. 259–267.

36. Thomas himself seems to hold, as in *On the Eternity of the World*, that it is creation in time and not creation *ex nihilo* which distinguishes the believer's understanding of the way in which the divine causality is exercised.

37. The point being made emerges from a number of texts when they are juxtaposed: *Summa theologiae*, IaIIae, q. 90, q. 94, and q. 100, articles, 1, 2, and 3.

38. " . . . that God exists and the other things known of God by natural reason, as suggested by Rom. 1:19–20, are not articles of faith, but preambles to the articles; faith presupposes natural knowledge as grace presupposes nature and (generally) perfection presupposes the perfectible." *Summa theologiae*, Ia, q. 2, a. 2, adlm.

39. I have in mind Kierkegaard's *Philosophical Fragments* (Princeton, 1962).

40. *Summa contra gentiles*, I,6.

41. *Summa theologiae*, IaIIae, q. 6, a. 1.

42. *Ibid.*

43. *Ibid.*, Ia, q. 2, a. 1, ad 2m.

44. *Ibid.*, Ia, q. 2, a. 3. I have added numbers to the text.

45. As by Alvin Plantinga in *God and Other Minds* (Ithaca, 1967).

46. One contemporary approach may be found in Alvin Plantinga, *The Nature of Necessity* (Oxford, 1974).

47. *Summa theologiae,* Ia, q. 1, a. 2.

48. Exposition of Boethius's *De trinitate*, q. 2, a. 3.

Selected Bibliography

A. Primary Sources

1. In Latin

Note: Good lists of Aquinas's works are provided by I. T. Eschmann, "A Catalogue of St. Thomas's Works: Bibliographical Notes," in Etienne Gilson, *The Christian Philosophy of St. Thomas Aquinas* (New York: Random House, 1956), pp. 381–439; and "A Brief Catalogue of Authentic Works," in James Weisheipl, *Friar Thomas D'Aquino* (New York: Doubleday, 1974), pp. 355–405.

Opera Omnia. Leonine Edition. Rome: Typographia Vaticana, 1882 ff. This edition is still incomplete, but the work goes on. Volume 47 of a projected 50 appeared in 1969.

Opera Omnia. New York: Benziger, 1948–50. 25 vols. [reprint of 1852–73 Parma edition].

In Aristotelis Librum De Anima Commentarium. Ed. Pirotta. Turin: Marietti, 1948.

In Aristotelis libros Peri Hermeneias et Posteriorum Analyticorum Expositio. Ed. Spiazzi. Turin: Marietti, 1955.

In Aristotelis libros De Coelo et Mundo, De Generatione et Corruptione, Meteorologicorum Expositio. Ed. Spiazzi. Turin: Marietti, 1952.

In Aristotelis libros De Sensu et Sensato, De Memoria et Reminiscentia Commentarium. Ed. Spiazzi. Turin: Marietti, 1949.

In Octo libros Physicorum Aristotelis Commentarium. Ed. Maggiolo. Turin: Marietti, 1954.

In Decem libros Ethicorum Aristotelis ad Nicomachum Expositio. Ed. Cathala. Turin: Marietti, 1949.

In Duodecem libros Metaphysicorum Aristotelis Expositio. Ed. Cathala and Spiazzi. Turin: Marietti, 1950.

Expositio super librum Boethii De Trinitate. Ed. Bruno Decker. Leiden: Brill, 1959.

In librum beati Dionysii De Divinis Nominibus. Ed. Pera. Turin: Marietti, 1950.

Super librum De Causis Expositio. Ed. H. D. Saffrey. Fribourg: Societé Philosophique, 1954.

Super Epistolas Sancti Pauli Lectura. Ed. Cai. 2 vols. Turin: Marietti, 1953.

Scriptum super libros Sententiarum Magistri Petri Lombardi. Ed. Mandonnet and Moos. 4 vols. Paris: Lethielleux, 1929.

Summa theologiae. Cura Fratrum Ordinis Praedicatorum. 5 vols. Madrid: Biblioteca de Autores Cristianos, 1955.

Summa Contra Gentiles. Editio Manualis Leonina. Rome: Marietti, 1946.

Compendium theologiae. Ed. Verardo. In *Opuscula Theologica,* Vol. 1. Turin: Marietti, 1954.

Quaestiones Quodlibetales. Ed. Spiazzi. Turin: Marietti, 1949.

Opusculum De Ente et Essentia. Ed. Sestili. Turin: Marietti, 1948.

Opusculum De Principiis Naturae. In *Opuscula Philosophica.* Ed. Spiazzi. Turin: Marietti, 1954.

Quaestiones Disputatae. Ed. Spiazzi, Pession, Calcaterra, Centi, Bazzi, Odetto. 2 vols. Turin: Marietti, 1949. Volume 1 contains the *De Veritate*; Volume 2 contains *De Potentia Dei, De Anima, De Spiritualibus Creaturis, De Unione Verbi Incarnati, De Malo,* and *De Virtutibus in Communi.*

Tractatus De Unitate Intellectus Contra Averroistas. Ed. Keeler. Rome: Gregorian University, 1946.

De Aeternitate Mundi Contra Murmurantes. In *Opuscula Philosophica.* Ed. Spiazzi. Turin: Marietti, 1954.

De Regimine Principum et De Regimine Judaeorum. Ed. Mathis. Turin: Marietti, 1948.

Super Evangelium S. Matthaei Lectura. Ed. Cai. Turin: Marietti, 1951.

Super Evangelium S. Ioannis Lectura. Ed. Cai. Turin: Marietti, 1952.

2. In English

Aristotle On Interpretation: Commentary by St. Thomas and Cajetan. Trans. Jean Oesterle. Milwaukee: Marquette University Press, 1962.

Commentary on the Posterior Analytics. Trans. F. R. Larcher. Albany: Magi, 1970.

Commentary on Aristotle's Physics. Trans. R. Blackwell et al. New Haven: Yale University Press, 1963.

Aristotle's De Anima with the Commentary of St. Thomas Aquinas. Trans. K. Foster and R. Humphries. New Haven: Yale University Press, 1951.

Commentary on the Metaphysics of Aristotle. Trans. J. P. Rowan. 2 vols. Chicago: Regnery, 1964.

Commentary on the Nicomachean Ethics. Trans. C. I. Litzinger. 2 vols. Chicago: Regnery, 1964.

The Trinity and the Unicity of the Intellect. Trans. R. E. Brennan. St. Louis: Herder, 1946.

Division and Methods of the Sciences. Trans. A. Maurer. Toronto: Pontifical Institute of Medieval Studies, 1953.

On the Unity of the Intellect Against the Averroists. Trans. B. Zedler. Milwaukee: Marquette University Press, 1968.

St. Thomas, Siger de Brabant, St. Bonaventure: On the Eternity of the World. Trans. E. Vollert, L. Kendzierski, and P. Byrne. Milwaukee: Marquette University Press, 1968.

Aquinas on Being and Essence. Translation and commentary by Joseph Bobik. Notre Dame: University of Notre Dame Press, 1965.

On the Principles of Nature. Trans. R. J. Henle and V. Bourke. St. Louis: St. Louis University, 1947.

Summa theologiae. Bilingual edition in 60 vols; executive editor, Thomas Gilby. New York: McGraw-Hill, 1964 ff.

On the Truth of the Catholic Faith (Summa Contra Gentiles). Trans. A. Pegis, J. F. Anderson, V. Bourke, C. O'Neil. 5 vols. Notre Dame: University of Notre Dame Press, 1976.

Compendium of Theology. Trans. Vollert. St. Louis: St. Louis University, 1947.

On Truth. Trans. R. Mulligan, B. McGlynn, R. Schmidt. 3 vols. Chicago: Regnery, 1952–54.

On the Power of God. Trans. L. Shapcote. Westminster, Md.: Newman Press, 1952.

On Spiritual Creatures. Trans. M. C. Fitzpatrick and J. J. Wellmuth. Milwaukee: Marquette University Press, 1951.

On the Soul. Trans. J. P. Rowan. St. Louis: Herder, 1949.

On the Virtues in General. Trans. J. Reid. Providence, 1951.

On Charity. Trans. L. Kendzierski. Milwaukee: Marquette University Press, 1960.

Commentary on St. Paul's Epistle to the Galatians. Trans. F. R. Larcher. Albany: Magi, 1966.

Commentary on St. Paul's Epistle to the Ephesians. Trans. M. L. Lamb. Albany: Magi, 1966.

Catena Aurea. Oxford: Oxford University Press, 1841–45.

Treatise on Separate Substances. Critical edition of the Latin text and English translation by Francis Lescoe. West Hartford, Conn., St. Joseph College Press, 1963.

B. *Secondary Sources*

ANDERSON, JAMES F. *The Bond of Being.* St. Louis: Herder, 1949.
A presentation of Thomas's teaching on analogy along Caje-
tanian lines, and a comparison with modern positions.

ARMSTRONG, R. A. *Primary and Secondary Precepts in Thomistic
Natural Law Teaching.* The Hague: Nijhoff, 1966. A good survey
of the major interpretations, with an excellent bibliography.

BOBIK, JOSEPH. *Aquinas On Being and Essence.* Notre Dame: University of Notre Dame Press, 1965. An excellent rethinking and
appraisal which sees this opusculum as a veritable summary of
Thomistic metaphysics.

BONNETTE, DENNIS. *Aquinas' Proofs for God's Existence.* The Hague:
Nijhoff, 1972. Argues for the centrality of the principle that the
per accidens implies the *per se.*

BOURKE, VERNON J. *Aquinas's Search For Wisdom.* Milwaukee: Bruce
1965. Essential. Alternating biographical and doctrinal chapters.

BURRELL, DAVID. *Analogy and Philosophical Language.* New Haven:
Yale University Press, 1960. An historical survey together with
an analysis of Thomas on analogy and an argument for its
continuing relevance.

————. *Exercises in Religious Understanding.* Notre Dame: University of Notre Dame Press, 1974. Chapter on Aquinas particularly interesting after earlier ones on Augustine and Anselm.

CAHN, STEVEN. *Fate, Logic and Time.* New Haven: Yale University
Press, 1967. Thomas and others on determinism.

CHENU, M. D. *A Guide to the Study of Thomas Aquinas.* Chicago:
University of Chicago Press, 1964. An excellent introduction
to Thomas and his works in their medieval setting.

CHESTERTON. G. K. *Saint Thomas Aquinas.* London: Hodder & Staugh-
ton, 1934. A delightful *tour de force* Etienne Gilson would have
liked to write.

CLARK, MARY T. *Aquinas Reader.* New York: Anchor, 1974. Selections wisely chosen and interestingly arranged.

COPLESTON, F. C. *Aquinas.* Baltimore: Penguin, 1970. Good introductory survey.

D'ARCY, ERIC. *Conscience and Its Right to Freedom.* London: Sheed
and Ward, 1961. Despite the title, a good general introduction
to Thomas's moral thought, with reference to recent controversies.

DEKONINCK, CHARLES. *Ego Sapientia: La Sagesse Qui Est Marie.*
Quebec: Presses Universitaires, 1943. A Thomist on Mariology.

————. *The Hollow Universe.* Oxford: Oxford University Press,

1960. A lucid and brief presentation of the Thomistic philosophy of nature.

————. *La Piété du Fils.* Quebec: Presses Universitaires, 1954. An essay on the Assumption.

————. *De la primauté du bien commun.* Quebec: Presses Universitaires, 1943. A polemic against some interpretations of the common good.

DOIG, JAMES. *Aquinas on Metaphysics.* The Hague: Nijhoff, 1972. An interpretation of Thomas's metaphysics with reference to his Arab and Latin interpreters.

FABRO, CORNELIO. *Esegesi Tomistici.* Rome: Lateran, 1969. A collection of Thomistic studies of extreme interest.

————. *Participation et Causalité.* Louvain: Nauelwaerts, 1961. *Sui generis* account of the significance of *esse* in the thought of Aquinas.

FOSTER, K. *The Life of St. Thomas Aquinas.* London: Newman, 1959.

GARRIGOU-LAGRANGE, R. *Reality: A Synthesis of Thomistic Thought.* St. Louis: Herder, 1960. Solid survey by an eminent Thomist.

GEACH, PETER. *God and the Soul.* New York: Schocken, 1969. Contains an important essay, "Form and Existence," in which Geach discusses Thomas's *esse* in the light of the denial that "exists" is a predicate, logically speaking.

————. *Mental Acts.* London: Routledge & Kegan Paul, 1957. A denial that Thomas is an abstractionist, in Geach's sense.

GEACH, PETER, and ANSCOMBE, ELIZABETH. *Three Philosophers.* Oxford: Blackwell, 1961. Essays on Aristotle, Aquinas, and Frege.

GILSON, ETIENNE. *Being and Some Philosophers.* Toronto: Pontifical Institute of Medieval Studies, 1952. A controversial insistence on the uniqueness of Thomas, marked perhaps by an excessive desire to drive a wedge between Aristotle and Aquinas.

————. *The Christian Philosophy of St. Thomas Aquinas.* New York: Random House, 1956. Gilson's *chef d'oeuvre,* which he has been revising over a long and distinguished career.

HENRY, D. P. *Medieval Logic and Metaphysics.* London: Hutchinson University Library, 1972. A discussion of some medieval tenets, notably the distinction of essence and existence, using the tools of modern logic, specifically Lesnieski's ontology.

JAFFE, H. *Thomism and Aristotelianism.* Chicago: University of Chicago Press, 1952. Argues on the basis of the *Nicomachean Ethics* and Thomas's commentary on it that Aristotle and Aquinas differ more than superficially on moral matters.

KENNY, A. *Aquinas: A Collection of Critical Essays.* New York: Anchor, 1969.

—————. *The Five Ways.* London: Schocken, 1969. Survey of the Thomistic proofs of God's existence and standard difficulties.

KING-FARLOW, JOHN and CHRISTENSEN, W. N. *Faith and the Life of Reason.* Dordrecht: Reidel, 1972. Includes discussion of Thomas on the notion of a just war.

KLUBERTANZ, GEORGE. *St. Thomas Aquinas and Analogy.* Chicago: Loyola University Press, 1960. Argues for a large number of types of analogy against a frieze of texts.

LYTTKENS, HAMPUS. *The Analogy Between God and the World.* Almqvist & Wiksells Boktryckeri, Uppsala, 1952. An early entry by a Protestant scholar in the recent upsurge of interest in Thomistic analogy.

MARITAIN, JACQUES. *The Angelic Doctor.* New York: Scribner's, 1958.

—————. *The Degrees of Wisdom.* New York: Scribner's, 1959. The ascending line of Thomas's thought from natural philosophy through metaphysics and theology to mysticism.

MASCALL, E. I. *Existence and Analogy.* Athlone Press, London, 1949. A popular work by an Anglican Thomist.

MCINERNY, RALPH. *The Logic of Analogy.* The Hague: Nijhoff, 1961. Argues that the doctrine of analogous naming is a logical doctrine in Thomas's sense; not an attack on metaphysics.

—————. *Thomism in an Age of Renewal.* New York: Doubleday, 1966.

MONDIN, B. *The Principle of Analogy in Protestant and Catholic Theology.* The Hague: Nijhoff, 1963.

—————. *Il Problema del Linguaggio Teologico.* Brescia: Queriniana, 1971. Remarkable for its range and depth.

NAUS, JOHN. *The Nature of the Practical Intellect According to St. Thomas Aquinas.* Rome: Gregorian, 1969. A careful and thorough treatment.

O'BRIEN, THOMAS. *Metaphysics and the Existence of God.* Washington: ACPA, 1960. Though not innovative, solid and interesting.

OWENS, JOSEPH. *The Doctrine of Being in the Aristotelian Metaphysics.* Toronto: Pontifical Institute of Medieval Studies, 1951. This landmark work attempts to go beyond the interpreters to Aristotle himself.

—————. *St. Thomas and the Future of Metaphysics.* Milwaukee: Marquette University Press, 1957.

PEGIS, ANTON. *Introduction to St. Thomas Aquinas.* New York: Modern Library, 1965. Texts from *Summa theologiae* and *Summa Contra Gentiles* illustrating the great themes of Thomas's thought.

PIEPER, JOSEF. *Belief and Faith.* New York: Pantheon, 1963. A rethinking of Thomas on faith, with reference to Newman.

————. *Guide to Thomas Aquinas.* New York: Pantheon, 1962. An informative and lyrical introduction.

————. *The Silence of St. Thomas.* New York: Pantheon, 1953. Meditative, suggestive: why did Thomas stop writing?

PLANTINGA, ALVIN. *The Nature of Necessity.* Oxford: Oxford University Press, 1974. Notable for its use of possible worlds semantics, this work provides an ingenious handling of the problem of evil.

PRELLER, V. *Divine Science and the Science of God.* Princeton: Princeton University Press, 1967. A familiar theme, but treated in such a way as to surprise the traditional Thomist.

PRIOR, A. N. *Papers on Time and Tense.* Oxford: Oxford University Press, 1968.

ROENSCH, F. J. *Early Thomistic School.* Dubuque: Priory Press, 1964. A corrective of prevailing modern views as to what questions were controverted in the early history of Thomism.

ROMMEN, H. *The Natural Law.* St. Louis: Herder, 1947. Still a basic work on the subject.

ROSS, J. F. *Inquiries into Medieval Philosophy.* Westport, Conn.: Greenwood, 1971. A remarkable collection of essays displaying analytic, logical or formalistic, and traditional approaches.

SILLEM, E. *Ways of Thinking About God.* New York: Sheed and Ward, 1961.

SIMON, YVES. *Introduction à l'Ontologie du Connaître.* Paris: Desclee de Brouwer, 1934. Both textually based and innovative.

WEISHEIPL, J. *Friar Thomas D'Aquino.* New York: Doubleday, 1974. The most recent and thorough introduction; first-rate, filled with provocative interpretations and resolutions.

Index

191